THE CHILDREN'S ILLUSTRATED
JEWISH BIBLE

THE CHILDREN'S ILLUSTRATED
JEWISH BIBLE

Stories retold by
LAAREN BROWN *and* LENNY HORT

Illustrated by
ERIC THOMAS

Consultants:
CANTOR DIANE DORF *and*
RABBI STEVEN MORGEN

DK PUBLISHING

Penguin Random House

2007 REVISED EDITION

Senior Editor Susan Reuben
Senior Art Editor Susan St. Louis
Editorial Assistant Lisa Stock
Managing Editor Camilla Hallinan
Publishing Manager Sunita Gahir
Category Publisher Andrea Pinnington
Producer, Pre-Production Robert Dunn
Senior Producer Jude Crozier
Additional illustrations Eric Thomas
Jacket Designer Priyanka Bansal

Editor's Note: The dates listed in this book are chronicled BCE,
meaning "Before the Common Era," and CE, meaning "Common Era."

Quotes from the Bible have been modernized from
The Holy Scriptures According to the Masoretic Text: A New Translation,
copyright © 1917 by The Jewish Publication Society of America, Philadelphia.

This American Edition, 2020
First American Edition, 1997
Published in the United States by DK Publishing
1450 Broadway, Suite 801, New York, New York 10018
(Some material in this book also appeared in The Children's
Illustrated Bible published in 1994, 2004)

Text copyright © 2007 Laaren Brown and Lenny Hort
Illustrations and compilation copyright © 1994, 1997, 2004, 2007, 2020
Dorling Kindersley Limited
DK, a Division of Penguin Random House LLC

20 21 22 23 24 25 10 9 8 7 6 5 4 3 2 1
001–316684–Feb/2020

A catalog record for this book
is available from the Library of Congress
ISBN: 978-1-4654-9106-0

DK books are available at special discounts when purchased in bulk for sales promotions,
premiums, fund-raising, or eductional use. For details, contact: DK Publishing Special Markets,
1450 Broadway, Suite 801, New York, New York 10018
SpecialSales@dk.com

Printed and bound in Hong Kong

A WORLD OF IDEAS:
SEE ALL THERE IS TO KNOW

www.dk.com

Foreword

by Laaren Brown and Lenny Hort

What does it mean to be Jewish? It means trying to be a good person, and treating everyone around you the way you would like to be treated, and working to make the world a better place, and trusting that God will be pleased with the way you live your life. Many people of other religions live by these same ideals. But being Jewish means something more, too. As Jews we are encouraged to think for ourselves, and we pass that way of thinking from generation to generation. Our rabbis and cantors, our parents and teachers urge us to think, to question, to look deeper and ask more, more, more.

The stories of the Bible are great stories—and one of the reasons they are so great is that they can be understood in many different ways and on many different levels. We read the stories in the Torah over again each year, so that as we grow up and change, we can see new questions in each story. Why does God tell Adam and Eve about one tree but not the other? Why does God save Noah and his family and the animals and no one else? Why does God ask Abraham to sacrifice his son? Every day, every week, Jewish children are encouraged to think about these stories for themselves and to ask questions.

To write the stories in this book, we looked at the Bible and then asked many, many questions. How? What? When? Who? And of course...why? Why, why, why? And why not?

We have retold these stories to show one way—our way—of telling each one. We have tried to put ourselves in the place of some of the great heroes and heroines of the Bible, and to ask ourselves how they might have felt in these amazing, challenging, exciting circumstances. Then we shared our answers with you. But there is no one right way to tell these stories, and there is no one right way to understand these stories.

Now it is your turn to ask.

CONTENTS

"*And you shall love the Lord your God with all your heart, and with all your soul, and with all your might. And these words, which I command you this day, shall be upon your heart; and you shall teach them diligently unto your children, and shall talk of them when you sit in your house, and when you walk by the way, and when you lie down, and when you rise up.*"

DEUTERONOMY 5–7

Introduction to the Bible

Torah
Torah scrolls are carefully handwritten on parchment by scribes. The writing, all 304,805 words of it, is checked and checked and checked again to make sure it is perfect.

The Bible is the great holy book of our people, the Jews. The Bible that we use in synagogue and at home is really a lot of short books put together so that we can have them all in one place. There are thirty-nine books in all, and scholars think that they were written by many different people over the course of hundreds of years.

These books tell us stories, provide laws and rules for us to follow, and offer bits of wisdom, prayers, and poetry. Some of the stories we all know very well, because rabbis and cantors, parents and teachers and everyone else talks about them all the time. You know about Moses and the plagues and the parting of the Red Sea. You know about Noah and the ark. You know about Esther and how she saved the Jews. But there are hundreds more great stories in the Bible, stories that tell us about God and about human nature.

In synagogue every Shabbat, we read a portion of the Torah, which is the first part of the Bible—traditionally, the part that Moses wrote down as God told the story to him. The Torah, also called the Five Books of Moses, consists of the first five books of the Bible: Genesis, Exodus, Leviticus, Numbers, and Deuteronomy. These books tell one long continuous story, from the Creation to the death of Moses. Then the Bible continues with thirty-four more books.

The Bible, or Tanakh, is the primary sacred text of our people. As Jews, we are commanded to study the Bible and to think about what it means. Discussing and interpreting and analyzing and even arguing about the possible meanings of each word—this debate is part of our heritage.

This new collection contains many of the great stories from the Torah and from the rest of the Bible, including tales about Abraham, Isaac, Jacob, and Joseph, Moses, Joshua, Ruth, Naomi, David, Solomon, Daniel, and Esther.

Moses received God's laws at Mount Sinai

Stories about kings, judges, and prophets, plus beautiful poetry and sayings are here—including some that you might have heard without knowing where they came from. The Bible is part of our everyday lives, because the great stories of the Bible are woven into literature and movies and TV shows, even everyday conversation. (Have you ever heard someone say, "We're going to have to build

A rabbi is a teacher. Rabbis help us learn and explore the Torah

To become a bar or bat mitzvah, a young person reads from the Torah.

an ark!" when it rains?)

Christians honor the books of the Tanakh, too. Their religion, like ours, is based on the belief in one all-powerful God, the creator of the universe. Sometimes you might hear what we call "the Bible" called the "Old Testament," because Christians also have another set of books they hold sacred, the teachings of Jesus Christ, which they call the "New Testament." But for Jewish people, the books of the Tanakh are the complete Bible.

The stories and ideas in the Bible have been handed down to us from ancient times. The Dead Sea Scrolls, discovered in caves near the Dead Sea in Israel, are a collection of very old parchment scrolls, many of which have crumbled into fragments. The oldest pieces date from the second century BCE. Scraps of almost every book in the Bible have been found among the Dead Sea Scrolls, which tells us that the words of God have been important to people for thousands of years.

Discovery
Long, long ago, the Dead Sea Scrolls were carefully stored in pottery jars, then placed in caves at Quman, near the Red Sea. They were rediscovered in 1947.

THE CHILDREN'S ILLUSTRATED
JEWISH BIBLE

*"In the beginning
God created the heaven
and the earth."*

GENESIS 1:1

Bible Lands

Most of the stories in the Bible take place in a small area near the Mediterranean Sea. Today, these places are called Israel, Lebanon, Jordan, and Egypt. Some, like Egypt, have had the same name since ancient times. Others have newer names. And Israel, our own homeland, was created as a country in 1948. It lies in the very place where Canaan, the Promised Land, was and the land where Abraham and his descendants lived.

Bible experts think that Abraham probably lived about 1800 BCE. In his time, and for hundreds of years after and before him, this land was green and lush. Years ago, Canaan was covered with trees, but as the area developed over the centuries, the trees were used for building and burning. Today, there is much more desert than there was in ancient days.

Then and now, the area had tall mountains and harsh deserts, the salty Dead Sea and the sparkling waters of the Mediterranean.

Many people like to remember special events in their lives by "planting a tree in Israel." They give money, and a tree is planted in the Holy Land. Trees that grew in biblical times and are still planted today include olive, pine, cypress, tamarisk, acacia, date palm, fig, myrtle, almond, oak, willow, poplar, and carob.

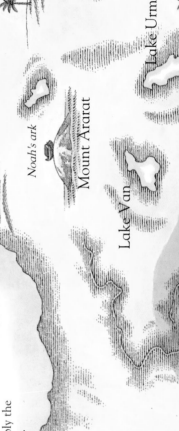

Black Sea

Noah's ark

Mount Ararat

Lake Van

Lake Urmia

ASSYRIA

Spring fields
Wildflowers like these grew in Canaan in ancient times. The Book of Deuteronomy lists seven plants special to the land of Israel: wheat, barley, grape vines, figs, pomegranates, olive trees, and honey—probably the sweet juice of dates.

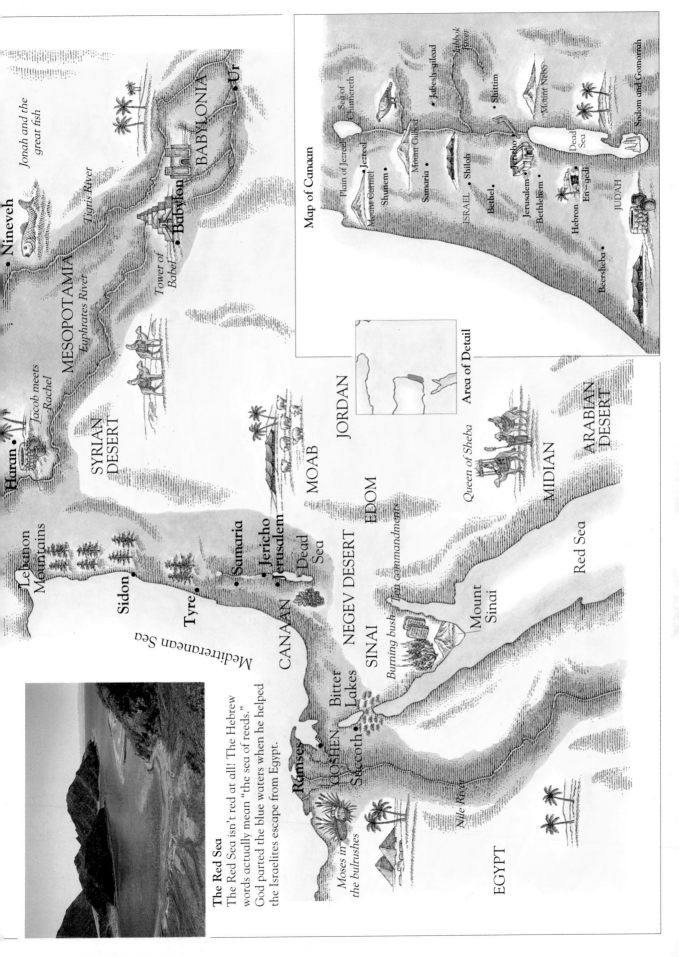

The Red Sea
The Red Sea isn't red at all! The Hebrew words actually mean "the sea of reeds." God parted the blue waters when he helped the Israelites escape from Egypt.

Map of Canaan

Tabernacles and Temples

Abraham

The people of Israel were the first to worship one God rather than many gods. That is the story the Bible tells—how God made His covenant with Abraham and his family. God says to Abraham, "I will make My covenant between Me and you...and you shall be the father of many nations."

Today, all Jews consider themselves to be descended from Abraham. Wherever there are Jews in this world, a little bit of the spirit of Abraham, and of the close link between God and Abraham, still lives.

On Mount Sinai, God gave the Ten Commandments to Abraham's descendant Moses. These commandments, or laws, tell the children of Israel how to behave and how to honor God. The Bible lists a total of 613 commandments, or mitzvot, to guide us. With these mitzvot, we worship God not just in synagogue, but every day, from morning to night, from night to morning.

According to the Torah, the Ten Commandments were carved onto two stone tablets by God, and these two tablets were the most sacred objects in existence. Moses smashed the original tablets when he came down from Sinai and found the Israelites worshiping the golden calf. But later he carved new tablets. They were kept in a beautiful box called the Ark of the Covenant.

The Ark of the Covenant held the tablets carved with the Ten Commandments.

THE TABERNACLE

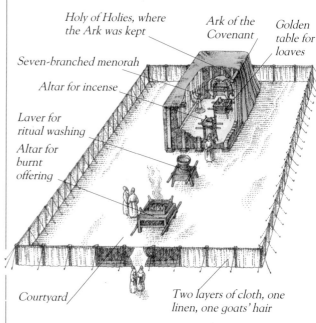

Holy of Holies, where the Ark was kept

Ark of the Covenant

Golden table for loaves

Seven-branched menorah

Altar for incense

Laver for ritual washing

Altar for burnt offering

Courtyard

Two layers of cloth, one linen, one goats' hair

As the Israelites traveled, the Ark traveled with them. In each new place, the people would set it in a special tent called a tabernacle, or, in Hebrew, the Mishkan—"God's dwelling place." Colorful cloth was hung on a wooden frame to make the tabernacle, and the space inside was divided into two areas. The smaller one was the Holy of Holies, where the Ark was kept. In the larger outer room, people met and prayed. Incense burned. A seven-branched menorah lit the room, and once a week, twelve loaves of bread were placed on the gold table.

The seven-branched menorah burned each night.

After King David captured the city of Jerusalem and made it the capital of his kingdom, he dreamed of building a temple in the city to hold the Ark safely. Years later, his son Solomon built a beautiful temple that was a wonder of its time. Solomon's temple is often called the First Temple, and Jews around the world remember it

THE FIRST TEMPLE

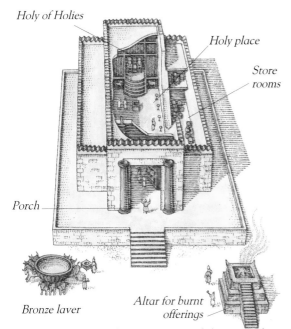

Holy of Holies

Holy place

Store rooms

Porch

Bronze laver

Altar for burnt offerings

as a symbol of one of our most joyful eras. The Temple was destroyed by the Babylonians in 586 BCE.

Another temple rose at the same place many years later, when the Persians allowed the Judeans to return to Jerusalem. It was near this building, often called the Second Temple, that Ezra read the Torah scrolls to the people. But by the time it was built in 515 BCE, the Ark of the Covenant and its tablets had disappeared completely.

Around 19 BCE, King Herod rebuilt and expanded the Second Temple, surrounding it with a large courtyard. The Western Wall in

Building the First Temple was Solomon's greatest achievement.

Jerusalem is a small part of the wall built by Herod to support the enormous platform on which the Temple stood. Today, Jews come from around the world to pray at this ancient

THE SECOND TEMPLE

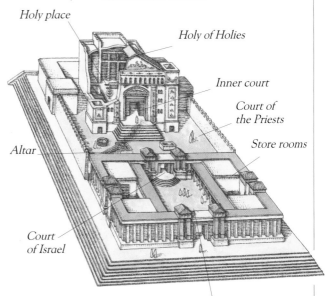

Holy place

Holy of Holies

Inner court

Court of the Priests

Store rooms

Altar

Court of Israel

Court of Women, where women prayed

site. Almost everyone writes a prayer on a tiny piece of paper and slips it into a crack in the wall, an act of faith that God will surely take note of its words.

The Western Wall is also called the Kotel.

The Creation

In the beginning, God created the heaven and the earth. Where there had been nothing, now there was something, unformed and empty, spinning in the darkness. And God said, "Let there be light." And there was light. God divided the light from the darkness, and called the light day, and the darkness He called night. There was evening and there was morning, and that made one whole day. The first day.

And God separated the waters of the earth from the waters of the sky, and He made the heavens. There was evening and there was morning, and that was the second day.

And God made the earth, and He gathered the water into seas, and He told the dry new land to bring forth grass and trees, fruit and seeds. The third day.

And God made the stars, to guide the way and to show the seasons, to give light to the earth. Then he made the Sun to rule over the day and the Moon to rule over the night. There was evening, and there was morning. The fourth day.

On the first day, God created light.

On the second day, God separated the waters of the earth and sky.

On the third day, God made the seas, the land, and all the plants.

Then God said, "Let the waters swarm with life, and the heavens fill with life." He made the fish in the sea and the birds in the sky. There was evening, and there was morning. The fifth day.

And God made all the animals of the earth. And He created man in His own image, to rule over the fish and the fowl and every living thing. There was evening, and there was morning. The sixth day.

The heavens and the earth were finished, and all of God's creations were done, ready to spin into the world we know. God saw that it was good. And the seventh day was blessed by God, for on that day He rested from the work He had done.

On the fourth day, God created the stars, the Sun, and the Moon.

On the fifth day, God made all the creatures of the sky and the sea.

On the sixth day, God made people and animals to live on His beautiful earth.

The Garden of Eden

Snake in the garden
Many people are frightened of snakes, like this Egyptian cobra, because of the way they look and because they can be poisonous. Did the snake's words "poison" Eve?

Cherubim
God sent cherubim, or cherubs, to guard the tree of life after Adam and Eve were cast out of the garden. In this Assyrian carving, cherubs were shown as winged lions with the heads of humans.

After He had formed man, and breathed life into him, God planted a beautiful garden in Eden. In the center of the garden, He placed two special trees—the tree of life, and the tree of the knowledge of good and bad.

He showed the lovely garden to the man, Adam. "Eat all you like from every tree—except for the tree of the knowledge of good and bad," God told him. "If you eat its fruit, you will die."

Once Adam was in the garden, it was clear to God that he would be lonely there. God brought all the beasts and the birds to Adam, and He gave him the job of naming them. But by the time he was done, God could see that none of the animals could be a true friend to Adam. So while Adam slept, God made a friend for him. Adam named her Eve.

Adam and Eve were naked, but the sun was warm, there was plenty to eat, and they were happy. Soon, though, the snake in the garden started giving Eve ideas. It said to her, "Doesn't that fruit on the tree of the knowledge of good and bad look tasty? Why not try it? It won't kill you, you know."

"God said it would," said Eve.

"God just doesn't want you to eat from that tree because then you would know the difference between good and bad, right and wrong," the

Adam and Eve were happy in the garden.

בְּרֵאשִׁית ב ג

Then Eve tasted the fruit from the tree of knowledge.

snake hissed. "Only God knows that. He wants to keep it to Himself."
The fruit did look tempting. Eve reached up and took a piece. She
hesitated only a moment before biting in. Then Adam took
a bite, too.

It was as if their eyes had been closed before, and now
they were suddenly open.

"You're naked!" cried Adam.

"You're naked, too!" said Eve. Quickly they
covered themselves with fig leaves.

When God came to the garden, Adam and Eve
hid from Him—for the first time ever. God knew
what had happened right away. "You disobeyed
me!" He said.

Then He thought, "If Adam and Eve ate
the fruit from the tree of life, they would never
die!" What could He do? He was angry, but
He still loved His children. So He gave
them clothes, to protect them from the cold
world outside, and then He cast them out
of the garden forever.

*God cast Adam and Eve out of the garden
to make their own way in the world.*

Cain and Abel

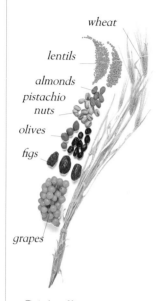

wheat

lentils

almonds

pistachio nuts

olives

figs

grapes

Cain's offering
Cain grew crops like the ones shown here. Why was God displeased with his offering? Maybe Cain did not give God the finest of his harvest.

Cain worked in the fields.

Abel was a shepherd.

Life was much harder for Adam and Eve outside the garden. They had to build a shelter. They had to hunt for food. They had to keep animals and grow crops. But they worked together to make their new life, and in time they had two sons, Cain and Abel.

Cain and Abel grew up, but they were very different. One day, Cain brought an offering to God, fruits and vegetables that he had grown. Abel also brought an offering, the finest new lambs from the flock he tended. God was very pleased with the lambs, but he ignored Cain and his gifts. Cain's face fell.

Abel's offering

Cain's offering

God preferred Abel's offering. Angry, Cain killed his brother.

God asked him why he was unhappy. "Surely, if you do right, that is a reward," He said. "But if you do not do right, sin waits for you. You make the choice."

Cain did not answer God. But later, when they were alone in the fields, Cain set upon Abel and killed him.

Soon enough, God said to Cain, "Where is Abel?"

Cain answered Him rudely. "I do not know. Am I my brother's keeper?"

"What have you done?" cried God instantly. "Your brother's blood cries out to me from the ground! From this moment on, Cain, you are banished from your home. You shall become a restless wanderer on this earth!"

Cain fell to his knees. "My punishment is too great to bear," he said. "If I am to wander alone always, anyone who meets me will be able to kill me."

"If anyone kills you, I will avenge you sevenfold," God told him. He put a mark on Cain, so that everyone who met him would know that he had God's protection—but they would know, too, that he had killed his own brother. And so Cain went out into the world, doomed always to wander alone.

Abel the shepherd
Abel would have spent all day, every day tending his flocks, leading them to green pastures. Only the plumpest lambs were chosen as offerings to God. The others provided wool, skins, meat, and milk for the family.

God condemns Cain to a life of lonely wandering.

Noah's Ark

More and more children were born, and they explored the world. But as they traveled on land and water, it seemed that they also traveled further and further from God's teachings. Their wickedness grew until God, with a heavy heart, knew that He must act. He saw that He would be forced to destroy His creations, the men and the women, the animals and the plants, and begin anew. "I will blot out everything on earth," He said.

Then God called on Noah, the one man He knew to be honest and true. He told Noah just how to build an ark, a sturdy ship that would carry Noah and his family through the heaviest rains and the harshest winds. "Build the boat of wood, and seal it with pitch on the inside and the outside," God told Noah. "Your ark must be very large,

Cypress trees
In ancient times, cypress trees grew all around the Bible lands. Cypress wood is light but strong—perfect for building a big boat like the ark.

With instructions from God, Noah and his sons built the ark.

Noah

"BUT I WILL ESTABLISH MY COVENANT WITH YOU; AND YOU SHALL COME INTO THE ARK, YOU, AND YOUR SONS, AND YOUR WIFE, AND YOUR SONS' WIVES WITH YOU."
GENESIS 6:18

בְּרֵאשִׁית ו ז

THERE WENT IN TWO AND
TWO UNTO NOAH INTO THE
ARK, MALE AND FEMALE, AS
GOD COMMANDED NOAH.
GENESIS 7:9

with three decks, so that there will be room inside for everything you will need to carry."

God told Noah to load the big new boat with food, for more than Noah's family would travel on this ark. Noah must also gather pairs, male and female, of every beast that walked the earth. "Birds of every kind, cattle of every kind, every creeping thing," God said. "Gather them all to you, and bring them inside the ark."

Noah did everything that God asked, and his wife and his three sons and their wives helped him,

The ark had room for all the animals.

Building a boat
Noah and his sons built the mighty ark all by themselves. To make the boat watertight, they would have coated the planks with tar. Today in the Middle East, some boats are still made in this traditional way.

because there was so much preparing to be done. First they had worked hard to build the ark, and now they worked hard to coax all the animals onto the ship, rushing faster and faster as the skies darkened above them. No sooner were the animals safely settled in the ark than the windows of heaven opened up. It rained.

The Flood

It rained and rained and rained, for forty days and forty nights. The waters rose up, and the ark traveled on and on through the endless sea. Noah and his family looked out at the strange new ocean, that covered their homes and their fields and everything that they had known before. There was no land to be seen anywhere. There were no other boats. There were no people, no birds, just water as far as the farthest horizon. And rain, falling in sheets, day after lonely day.

At last the rain ended, and the waters seemed a little lower. The ark came to rest on Ararat, at the very peak of the great mountain, which looked like a tiny island in a giant ocean. Noah opened the window of the ark, closed for so long to keep

The Flood
God saved Noah and his family and the animals. But every other living thing drowned in the flood, as artist Gustave Doré shows above.

AND THE WATERS PREVAILED, AND INCREASED GREATLY UPON THE EARTH; AND THE ARK WENT UPON THE FACE OF THE WATERS.
GENESIS 7:18

the rain out, and released one of the ark's ravens, a bird as black as a stormy sky. The raven flew and flew and then came back to the ark. There was nowhere else for it to go, no bit of land anywhere, just water.

Then Noah released a dove, white as the sun glowing on a summer day. After long searching, the dove came back to the ark and landed on Noah's outstretched hand. The dove had not rested in all that time—there was nowhere it could rest the sole of one foot, nowhere it could stop for even a moment.

For seven days, Noah comforted the dove. Then he sent it into the air again. This time, the dove returned to the ark that very evening, carrying a leaf from an olive tree. Now Noah knew that the waters were falling and that land, dry land with trees and plants, was near. He kept the dove for seven more days, then let her go, and he never saw that dove again. It had found a new home.

"Go forth from the ark," God told Noah, and he did, along with his wife and his sons and their wives, and all the animals that had been on the ark all those many days and nights, and all the new little animals that had been born and started to grow up right on the ark.

Noah built an altar and burned an offering to show how grateful he was that God had spared him and his family. As the smoke from the fire rose to God, His heart warmed toward His creations. He made a promise there and then: "While the earth remains, seedtime and harvest, and cold and heat, and summer and winter, and day and night shall not cease." Then God told Noah, "When a rainbow appears in the clouds, I will see it. And I will remember that I have made this promise, to protect all My creatures on earth."

Mount Ararat
The ark came to rest on Mount Ararat, in the mountainous part of what is now Turkey. Some people think that there may be some part of the ark still left in the mountains.

AND THE DOVE CAME IN TO HIM AT EVENTIDE; AND LO IN HER MOUTH AN OLIVE LEAF FRESHLY PLUCKED; SO NOAH KNEW THAT THE WATERS WERE ABATED FROM OFF THE EARTH.
GENESIS 8:11

The waters rose for forty days and forty nights.

The rainbow would always remind God of His promise to protect His creatures.

27

Genesis 11

The Tower of Babel

In the early days, everyone on God's earth spoke the same language and used the same words. Of course, this made it very easy for everyone to understand what everyone else was saying. Men and women slowly moved more and more to the east—why not? The land there was sunny and pleasant.

After they had found a nice new place to live, the people started to make bricks. And they began to build with the bricks. They made sturdy homes and strong buildings. Then one day, someone said, "Come, let us build

Babylon
Babel is traditionally thought to be the ancient walled city of Babylon, the capital of the empire of Babylonia. In Hebrew, the word for confusion is "bilbul." Say it out loud. Doesn't it sound like Babel?

The people of Babel built a tower to reach into the sky.

Tar for mortar

Mud bricks

28

a city, and a tower with its top in the sky. Everyone will be amazed by it!" So work began at once on a tall, tall tower that would reach right up to Heaven.

God came down from on high to take a look at the mighty tower. He was not happy. "How dare they?" He said. "They think that reaching up to the sky will make them equal to Me!" How could God teach the workers that He alone was the ruler of the universe?

Suddenly, down on the earth where the tower was rising, one man said to another, "Hand me that brick will you?" But to the other man, those words sounded like, "Na l'–ha–vir li et ha–l'–vei–nah, be–va–ka–shah?"

No one could understand anyone else! And now that they did not all speak the same language, the people became confused. They fought. They argued. They talked louder and louder, and a babble of noise rose up to God. But still they could not understand one another. Finally they stopped building their tall tower and they stopped building their great city, and they started moving out and away, all over the earth.

Ziggurat
The tower of Babel may have been a ziggurat, a temple tower that looks almost like a giant staircase. In ancient times, ziggurats had outside staircases that led up and up to a temple at the very top. There, it was thought, worshippers could be closer to God.

Building came to a sudden halt when everyone spoke different languages.

Mud bricks
The tower of Babel would have been made of many, many mud bricks. To make the bricks, mud and straw were mixed together, then formed and left to bake in the hot sun. In parts of the Middle East, mud bricks are still made in the same way today.

The Patriarchs

God promised Abraham that He would make Abraham's descendants as countless as the stars in the sky. "I will make nations of you, I will make kings come from you," God said. Abraham was already an old man, with no children, so he was amazed to hear God say that! But God did it. Abraham's line was carried on by his son Isaac, then by Isaac's son Jacob. And Jacob continued the line with his many sons—twelve of them.

These men, Abraham, Isaac, and Jacob, are our patriarchs. That means that they are the fathers of our whole family of Jews. Our family has matriarchs, too, of course—Sarah, Rebekah, and Rachel and Leah. A patriarch or matriarch leads his or her family. In your own family, you might have a father or a mother, a grandfather or a grandmother, a great-uncle or a great-aunt or a great-great-grandfather who is considered a patriarch or a matriarch to all of the younger relatives.

Just like those older relatives, so Abraham, Isaac, and Jacob are the leaders of the whole family of Jews, all around the world.

Abraham waited a long time to start becoming a patriarch, because he was an old man when he finally became a father, first to Ishmael, then to Isaac.

THE PATRIARCHS' FAMILY TREE

Abraham was the first of the patriarchs. Married to Sarah, he had a son with her servant, Hagar. Later Sarah gave birth to Isaac.

Abraham's son, Isaac, married Rebekah. Her brother, Laban, was the father of Leah and Rachel. They married Isaac's son Jacob.

Jacob was tricked into marrying Leah. Later he married her sister, Rachel, the woman he really loved.

Jacob had twelve sons and a daughter by his wives and their servants, Zilpah and Bilhah. In time, descendants of each of the sons became a tribe of Israel.

Sarah m. Abraham   Hagar

Isaac m. Rebekah   Laban   Ishmael

Esau   Jacob m. Leah and Rachel   Zilpah   Bilhah

Reuben Simeon Levi Judah Issachar Zebulun Dinah   Joseph Benjamin Gad   Asher   Dan   Naphtali

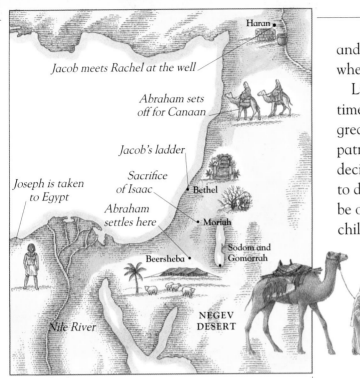

Jacob meets Rachel at the well

Haran

Abraham sets
off for Canaan

Jacob's ladder

Sacrifice
of Isaac

Bethel

Joseph is taken
to Egypt

Abraham
settles here

Moriah

Beersheba

Sodom and
Gomorrah

Nile River

NEGEV
DESERT

Patriarch places
Though there were towns in Canaan, the families of
Abraham, Isaac, and Jacob moved from place to place,
living in tents. This map shows some of the places
where the Bible stories about the patriarchs happened.

When at last Isaac was born, Abraham knew
that God had kept His promise to give him
children and a long line of descendants. God
asked some strange and even disturbing things
of Abraham, but Abraham trusted in God, no
matter what He asked. Isaac also trusted
God, and God made the
same promise to Isaac
that his offspring
would be numberless
as the stars. Jacob
had a dream about a
ladder reaching right
up to God in Heaven,

Desert life
Abraham, Isaac, and Jacob
probably lived nomadic
lives, moving wherever the
grazing was best for their
animals and they could
live in peace. Their homes
probably looked much like
these Bedouin tents.

and he trusted God and marked the spot
where he had slept as a holy place.

Like all fathers, especially in biblical
times, Abraham, Isaac, and Jacob had
great power over their own families. The
patriarch was in charge of all family
decisions, including the ones that had
to do with worship, and his word had to
be obeyed. When he honored one of his
children with a blessing, that honor could
not be taken away—which is why Jacob
became Isaac's heir after Isaac
blessed him, even though Jacob
had tricked him.

When Jacob returned from his
uncle Laban's home with all his
children and prepared to face his
brother Esau many years after cheating
him, he wrestled with an angel all night.
In the morning, the angel told him that
his name would now be Israel—"the one
who struggles with God." And so today the
country of Israel is named after Jacob, and
the name is a reminder of our own struggles
and triumphs.

Abram's Journey

God told Abram to leave his home and to journey into the world, to a new land that God would show him. "I will make of you a great nation, Abram," said God, "and I will bless you. I will make your name great, and your name shall be a blessing forever."

As God had asked him, Abram took his wife, Sarai, and his brother's son, Lot, and everything they owned, and they all set out for the land of Canaan, the land God had promised to Abram. Abram was an old man when he left his comfortable

Abram's journey
This map shows the route Abram probably took on his journey from Ur, where he was born and lived for many years, to Canaan. Lot settled in Sodom.

Lot's people

There was not enough grazing for all the animals, so Lot and Abram parted ways.

Lot   *Abram*

Treasures from Ur
This golden helmet, and the dagger and its decorative sheath, were discovered in what was once the powerful city-state of Ur.

home in Haran, but he went willingly because God had chosen him. They traveled to Canaan, day after dusty day, and when they arrived Abram set up an altar to honor God. They traveled on and on, and God told them that all this land would be theirs forever.

But Abram had cattle, as well as gold and silver and tents and rugs and pots and servants and camels and donkeys, and Lot had cattle, as well as a whole caravan of his own, and there was not enough grazing for all the many, many animals. So

Abram stayed where he was, in the land of Canaan, and Lot traveled east, with his caravan trailing behind him, and he settled in Sodom.

And God said to Abram, after Lot had gone on his way, "Raise your eyes and look out from where you are, to the north and the south, to the east and the west, for I give all the land that you see to you and your children, forever."

Abram settled down in the new land. Time went by, and then God came to him in a vision. "I give you My strength, Abram," God told him. "Your reward shall be very great."

"God, how great can You make my reward?" Abram asked, for he had been thinking about what God had told him earlier. "You have granted me no offspring, and when I die, there will be no one to mourn me."

IN THAT DAY THE LORD MADE A COVENANT WITH ABRAM, SAYING, "UNTO YOUR PEOPLE HAVE I GIVEN THIS LAND, FROM THE RIVER OF EGYPT UNTO THE GREAT RIVER, THE RIVER EUPHRATES."
GENESIS 15:18

Abram's people

Sarai

"Look up, Abram. Look toward the heavens," said God. "Your offspring shall number like the stars in the sky."

Abram believed God, but he was already an old man. Where would these multitudes of children come from?

Then God continued. "Know this, Abram. Your offspring will be strangers in a strange land, and they will be slaves, cruelly driven for four hundred years. But then I will judge the nation they have served. And in the end, Abram, I promise you, your people will be free. I have chosen them as My own."

The sun went down, and night fell. As Abram watched the starry skies, a flaming torch blazed through the night, the symbol of God's promise, His covenant with Abram and Abram's children to come.

Desert nomads
Abram and his family were nomads, traveling from place to place as they looked for grazing land and water for their animals. They carried everything they owned on camels, and they lived in tents that could be packed up and moved easily.

33

Abraham and Sarah

Living in tents
The deserts of the Middle East are still home to many people who live much like Abram, Lot, and Sarai. Because these Bedouin are constantly on the move, taking their flocks to fresh grazing, everything they own must be lightweight and easy to pack and carry. This tent is made of woven goat hair, which is naturally waterproof.

Ten years went by. Abram was very old now, and Sarai, his wife, still had not given him children. Abram knew that God had promised him sons, but where would they come from? He worried, and he worried more and more as the time passed.

"God has not given us children," Sarai said to him at last. "Try to have a child with Hagar, my maid. Perhaps she will have a son for us."

Soon Hagar knew that she would have a child, and she became very unkind to Sarai. Sarai was angry with Hagar and upset with her husband, and she told Abram that he would have to choose between Hagar and Sarai herself. "Hagar is your maid, Sarai," said Abram. "Do what you think best."

Sarai did not send Hagar away, but she treated her so harshly that Hagar ran away from their home, determined to bear her child alone. But she had not gone far when an angel called her by name. "Hagar, where have you come from, where are you going?"

"I am running away," Hagar told the angel.

"Go back to your mistress, though she is cruel to you," said the angel. "You will have a son, and you will

Hagar, expecting Abram's child, was rude to Sarai.

Alone in the desert, Hagar wept at Sarai's cruelty.

call him Ishmael. He will be a wild man, his hand against every man, and every man's hand against him. He will struggle."

Hagar did go back to Sarai. And when Hagar's son Ishmael was born, Abram was eighty-six years old, a new father for the first time. More time passed, and Abram was a very, very old man when God appeared to him once more.

Abram threw himself on the ground before God, and heard these words: "This is My covenant with you: You shall be the father of nations."

Abram said nothing, and God continued. "You shall no longer be called Abram, but Abraham, and your wife will not be called Sarai, but Sarah. Through the generations, your sons must be circumcised at eight days of age, as the mark of My covenant with you. And I will bless Sarah. I will give you a son by her."

"Can a child be born to a man a hundred years old, or a woman of ninety?" thought Abraham, laughing to himself. It was a strange idea. But he did not question God any more. "Lord," he said, "please favor Ishmael, my son."

"Sarah will bear you a son," repeated God. And since Abraham had laughed, He told him to name his son after the word for laughter. God said, "You will name him Isaac, and I will keep my covenant with him and his offspring."

"As for Ishmael, I have heeded you, and I will bless him," continued God. "But my covenant will be kept with Isaac, who Sarah will bear at this season next year." Then He was gone.

Mother and child
The ancient Israelites considered children to be a gift from God, and they cherished them, just as this Bedouin woman cherishes her little one. Sarai would have been very sad that she had never had a baby. Abram and Sarai must have been overjoyed at God's promise that He would make them parents.

Hagar　　*Abram*

After returning home, Hagar gave birth to her son, Ishmael.

Abraham and Sarah welcomed the three travelers.

Abraham

Sarah

Sarah laughed when she heard the men say that she would bear a son.

milk

bread

meat

curds

Desert meal
What did Sarah feed her visitors? Most meals would have included flat bread and milk from a goat or a sheep. Roasted meat and sour-milk curds might have rounded out the menu. Serving meat and milk together was not prohibited until after Moses's time.

Abraham did as God had told him, and all the men and boys of the household were circumcised. Soon after, as Abram sat in the shade outside his tent, three men, traveling through the desert, suddenly stood before him in the heat of the day. Quickly he rose to greet them.

"Please wait here and rest," Abraham said, and he ran to fetch cool water and the finest food. As they ate, Abraham realized that these were no ordinary travelers. One told him, "I will return here next year. And when I come back, Sarah will have a son."

Sarah, listening at the entrance of the tent, thought to herself, "Shall I bear a child, old as I am?" Just the idea was funny to her, as it had been to Abraham, and she laughed out loud, with surprise and with joy.

"Why did Sarah laugh?" said God, hearing her. "Is anything too wonderful for the Lord?"

36

Sodom and Gomorrah

Abraham's visitors, the two angels, journeyed on toward Sodom and Gomorrah. Abraham walked with them, to set them off on their journey. As they walked, God reflected on His promise to Abraham.

"Abraham is to be the father of nations," God thought to Himself. "Is it right that I should hide from him what I am about to do?" So when the angels had walked on, God said, "Abraham, the people of Sodom and Gomorrah have sinned greatly. I will judge them, whether they should live or die."

Upset, Abraham said, "But what if there are even fifty innocent people among them? Will you sweep away the innocent with the guilty?"

"If I find within the city of Sodom fifty innocent people, I will forgive the whole city for their sakes," said God.

"And what if the fifty should lack five? Will you destroy the whole city for want of the five?" said Abraham.

"I will not destroy the city if I find forty-five innocent people there," God said. Back and forth Abraham went with God, bargaining for the city of Sodom—what if there were but forty

AND GOD SAID, "VERILY, THE CRY OF SODOM AND GOMORRAH IS GREAT, AND, VERILY, THEIR SIN IS EXCEEDING GRIEVOUS. I WILL GO DOWN NOW."
GENESIS 18:20–21

Lot tried to calm the crowd.

Lot

An angry mob raged outside Lot's house, demanding the travelers.

innocent people? Thirty? Twenty? What if there were ten innocent people in all of Sodom, would God sacrifice them as He destroyed the city? At last God agreed. If Abraham could find even ten innocent souls in the whole of Sodom, God would spare the city.

Soon after this, God's angels approached the city of Sodom, and they passed Lot, sitting at the gate. "Please," he said, "rest and eat in my home, I welcome you."

They thanked him and went inside. But before they could rest, a huge mob of angry townspeople surrounded the house. Lot went out to reason with them, and he refused to give them the travelers. The crowd became angrier still. They pushed Lot, and started to push in his door—but the angels pulled him inside, and a dazzling white light blinded the mob.

"Quickly," the angels told Lot, for they knew now that there were not even ten innocent people in all of Sodom and Gomorrah. "Gather your family, for the Lord is about to destroy this city!" Lot ran to the homes of his married daughters and their husbands, and tried to persuade them to escape—but they laughed at him and would not come.

"Quickly!" the angels cried.

Cities by the sea
Sodom and Gomorrah may have been at the southern end of the Dead Sea, where the land was dry and fertile. Some experts think that an earthquake caused the sea to spread, covering the towns.

Dead Sea

Sodom and Gomorrah

•Zoar

God rained fire and brimstone down on Sodom and Gomorrah.

"Take your wife and your two youngest daughters, or all of you will be swept away as the city is destroyed." It was almost more than Lot could bear to leave the rest of his family behind, but the angels seized his hand, and the hands of his wife and young daughters, and they pulled them outside the city.

"Run!" they told the family. "Run for your lives, and do not look back!"

As she looked back at the destruction, Lot's wife was turned into a pillar of salt.

Only Lot and two of his daughters survived the disaster.

Then Lot and his wife and two daughters ran. They ran like they had never run before and never would run again, and Lot and his daughters did not look back. But Lot's wife did look back, to see her home one more time. And she was turned into a pillar of salt, standing alone forever in the desert.

And still Lot and the two girls ran. As the sun rose, they entered the little city of Zoar, while God rained fire on Sodom and Gomorrah. The fire destroyed the towns and everything around them, and it raged on all day and into the night.

The next morning, as Abraham stood in the place where he had begged God to spare the innocent, he looked out over the vast plain and the land where those cities had stood, and he saw the smoke rising from the land like the smoke of a kiln. Sodom and Gomorrah, and all the people who had lived there, were gone.

Pillars of salt
The Dead Sea is so salty that nothing can survive in the water. That is why it's called the Dead Sea. These salt deposits serve as a reminder of the terrible fate suffered by Lot's wife.

Abraham's Two Sons

Just as God had promised, and just at the time He had promised, Sarah bore a son for Abraham. Surely there had never been such a wonderful child! Abraham was one hundred years old that year, and Sarah was ninety, and never were new parents so very proud of a baby.

They named the boy Isaac, and Abraham kept his covenant with God by circumcising him when he was eight days old. A few months went by, and when Isaac was weaned, his parents gave a big feast in their little son's honor, and they invited everyone from far and away to celebrate with them.

Isaac was a sweet child, and Abraham and Sarah were overjoyed

Isaac

Ishmael

After Sarah had Isaac, she wanted Abraham to send Ishmael and Hagar away.

Abraham gave bread and water to Hagar, telling her to take Ishmael and go into the desert.

Water bearer
Hagar would have traveled with a light, strong water skin like this one, made from animal hide.

by their little boy, a miraculous gift from God in their old age. "Who would have thought that I would give Abraham a child at last?" said Sarah. "God has brought me laughter, and everyone who hears me laughs with me!"

But the more Sarah adored Isaac, the meaner she became about Ishmael. "Cast out that slave woman and her son," she ordered Abraham. "I will not have him sharing in Isaac's inheritance."

Distressed, Abraham asked God what he should do, for he loved his son Ishmael almost as much as he loved Isaac. "I will see that Ishmael is treated fairly," God told Abraham. "Do as Sarah asks, for it is true that your line shall be continued though Isaac."

Early the next morning, Abraham gave bread and water to Hagar and sent her away with young Ishmael. The mother and son wandered in the desert, and all too soon there was no bread for them to eat and no water for them to drink.

Hagar despaired. She put her little boy, weak and sobbing, in what little shade she could find under a bush, and she slipped away. "I cannot watch my child die," she thought, and then she wept, too.

God heard Ishmael crying. One of His angels called down to Hagar from Heaven and said, "Do not fear, Hagar. God has heeded the cry of your little boy. Come, lift him up and hold him by the hand, for God will make a great nation of him."

Hagar opened her eyes, and there before her was a well of fresh, cool water. She filled her waterskin and ran to her child, her Ishmael, and poured the water into his mouth.

Ishmael's People
The Arab people are traditionally believed to be descended from Ishmael.

An angel appeared to Hagar.

Ishmael opened his eyes, and he lived. He grew up to be a fine, strong man, a hunter and a warrior, for God was with him, in the desert on that day his mother thought would be his last, and always after.

Hagar saved Ishmael with water from the well.

The Sacrifice of Isaac

Desert hills
Abraham and Isaac traveled through the Negev Desert on their way to Moriah, where Abraham was to sacrifice his son.

God put Abraham's faith to the test. He said, "Abraham." Abraham answered, "Here I am."

God said to him, "Take your son, your favored one, Isaac, and offer him as a sacrifice."

Abraham did not question God. Early the next morning, he saddled his mule and loaded it with firewood for the burnt offering. He called for two servants and his son. They set off for a place that God would show them, the place where Abraham would sacrifice Isaac, because God had told him to.

They traveled for three days. Then Abraham took the wood and a firestone and a knife, and he and his son walked on together.

"Father!" said Isaac.

"Yes, my son," said Abraham.

"Father, here are the firestone and the wood, but where is the lamb for the burnt offering?" said Isaac.

"God will see to the lamb, my son," Abraham told him. Together they walked.

When they arrived at the place God had chosen, Abraham built an altar there and laid out the wood for a fire. Then he bound his son and laid him on the altar, on top of the wood.

And he picked up the knife to slay his son. Did his hand tremble? Was Isaac afraid? Closer and closer went Abraham's hand to Isaac's throat.

"Abraham! Abraham!" called an angel of God from above.

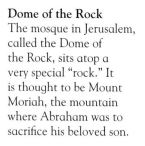

Dome of the Rock
The mosque in Jerusalem, called the Dome of the Rock, sits atop a very special "rock." It is thought to be Mount Moriah, the mountain where Abraham was to sacrifice his beloved son.

The servants waited with the donkey.

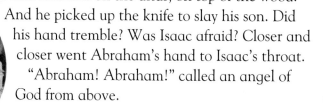

Abraham and Isaac went up the mountain to offer a sacrifice to God.

"Here I am," said Abraham, his eyes still cast down upon his son, bound on the altar.

"Do not raise your hand against the boy," said God through the angel. "For now I know that you fear God, since you have not withheld your son, your favored one, from Me."

Rams in the thicket
Abraham saw a ram, a male sheep, in the thicket, and he sacrificed it in place of Isaac. Rams' horns sometimes get tangled in bushes as the animals graze.

God's angel stopped Abraham from killing his son.

Abraham caught a ram and sacrificed it.

Abraham looked up. Were there tears in his eyes? He saw a ram, and so he made that his burnt offering, in place of his beloved son.

And God said, "I will bestow my blessing upon you and make your descendants as many as the stars of heaven and the sands on the seashore, and they shall seize the gates of your foes. All the nations of the earth shall bless you, because you have obeyed My commands."

Blessed by God, Abraham and Isaac left that place, and together they traveled home.

"IN BLESSING I WILL BLESS YOU, AND IN MULTIPLYING I WILL MULTIPLY YOUR PEOPLE AS THE STARS OF THE HEAVEN, AND AS THE SAND WHICH IS UPON THE SEASHORE."
GENESIS 22:17

Isaac and Rebekah

Rebekah offered water to Abraham's servant and to his camels.

At the well
Women often had to fetch the water for their families. They carried it home from community wells, usually located just outside the gates of the city.

Abraham was an old, old man now, and God had watched over him for all his long years. Abraham longed for one thing more, though—to see his son Isaac happy. He summoned his most trusted servant. "Go to the land of my birth, and find a wife for Isaac," he said.

That very day, the servant set out with a caravan of camels. He traveled to the city of Nahor, arriving at the time of evening when the women of the town came out to fetch water. "O Lord," he prayed, "God of my master, grant me good fortune this day. Let the maiden who gives water to me and to my camels be the wife You have chosen for Isaac."

Just then, a beautiful young woman came to the well. "Please," the servant said to her. "Let me sip a little water from your jar."

"Drink," she said sweetly. "And then I will draw water for your camels." And as the servant watched, she filled her jar again and again. So beautiful, so kind; was she the one? The servant spoke to her, asking her about herself and her family—and he was happy and astounded to discover that she was one of Abraham's people, the daughter of Abraham's own brother. "Surely God

Camels
Abraham's large herd of camels was a sign of his family's wealth. Camels are working animals, able to carry hundreds of pounds of supplies across the desert for hour after hour.

Isaac looked up and saw Rebekah for the first time.

is guiding me!" he thought.

Then he said, "Does your family have room for a traveler? Take these gifts, and find out for me." The maiden ran ahead with the heavy gold arm bands and a gold nose ring, and her brother Laban came out to welcome the servant. The servant could not rest until he had told his tale, how Abraham had been blessed by the Lord, how he wanted a wife for his son, how the servant had been guided by God to find Rebekah by the well.

"Then I bowed low before the Lord," the servant concluded, "for He had guided me to find the daughter of my master's brother for his son. Will she return to Abraham's home with me?"

"God has decided," answered Rebekah simply.

And the next day, the women of the household gathered around Rebekah and blessed her, singing, "O sister! May you grow into thousands of myriads." Then she set off to meet her husband, with Abraham's servant beside her.

As the caravan approached Abraham's house, Rebekah saw Isaac from afar. She drew up her veil, and as Isaac approached, their eyes met for the first time.

Nose ring
Abraham's servant gave Rebekah a nose ring to show to her father. It may have looked like the elaborate ring that this Bedouin woman is wearing.

Esau and Jacob

Isaac and Rebekah were married for many years, but they had no children. Isaac pleaded with God, and soon they knew that Rebekah would have a baby at last. But Rebekah could feel that something was wrong, that there was a struggle going on within her body. "Why, God?" she asked, deeply troubled.

"Two nations are in your womb," God said. "Two separate peoples shall issue from your body. One people shall be mightier than the other, and the older shall serve the younger."

When the time came, Rebekah did have two babies, twin boys. The firstborn baby was fuzzy with red hair all over; his parents named him Esau. The second to arrive was Jacob. Their mother gazed at her new babies, remembering what God had told her and wondering, as all mothers wonder, what the future would hold for them.

When the boys grew up, Esau became a skilled hunter; he was Isaac's favorite. Jacob, Rebekah's favorite, was thoughtful and resourceful. One day Esau came in from the hunt and saw that Jacob was cooking lentil stew. "I'm starving," said Esau. "Give me some stew, or I will drop dead right here and now."

Ibex
Esau would have hunted for game animals such as ibex. Ibex are related to goats, and their tasty meat was highly prized.

Esau, Isaac's favorite, was a hunter.

Jacob, Rebekah's favorite, preferred studying at home.

Esau traded his birthright for a plate of stew.

"First sell me your birthright," said Jacob.

"I am dying of hunger!" said Esau. "What good will my birthright be to me when I am dead?" And so he sold his birthright, his right as firstborn to Isaac's good name and property. Now Jacob, not Esau, would inherit those things from his father.

When Isaac was old and his eyes were too dim to see, he called for Esau to go hunting and prepare the meat for him. Then Isaac would give his firstborn son his final blessing, a gift from his father and from God, too.

Rebekah heard what Isaac said, and as soon as Esau was gone, she called for Jacob. "Quickly!" she told him. "You will serve your father, and receive his blessing instead of your brother."

"But Esau is hairy, and I am not," said Jacob. "My father will know I am not Esau as soon as he touches me. Then his curse will be upon me, not his blessing."

"His curse will be upon me!" said his mother. "Do as I say!" Quickly she prepared a rich meal of goat stew, and she covered Jacob with the goat's skin. Then he went to his father.

"Father," he whispered. "It is me, Esau. I have brought the food you asked for."

Lentil stew
Hungry Esau sold his birthright to his brother in exchange for "a mess of pottage." Pottage was made by cooking red lentils down into a thick stew. To eat it, diners scooped up the stew in thin pieces of bread.

Rebekah discovered that Isaac planned to give Esau his blessing.

So she helped Jacob to disguise himself as his brother.

And then Isaac, on his deathbed, gave his blessing to Jacob instead of Esau.

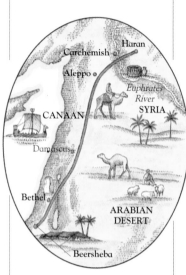

Jacob's journey
Jacob set off from Beersheba in southern Canaan. He stopped at Bethel, where God appeared to him in a dream. From there he may have followed the route of the trade caravans and passed through major cities, such as Damascus, before reaching Haran.

"Let me touch you." Isaac wondered. "The voice is the voice of Jacob...but the hands are the hands of Esau." The son before him even smelled like Esau, of the fields and the hunt. So Isaac blessed him, saying, "May God give you all the best of this earth. Let peoples and nations bow to you; let even your mother's sons bow down to you. Cursed be they who curse you, and blessed be they who bless you."

No sooner had Jacob left than Esau returned from hunting. He and Isaac quickly realized what had happened, how Jacob had deceived Isaac. Tears streaming down his face, Esau said, "Have you no blessing for me, Father?"

"I have made him master over you," said Isaac. "What can I do for you, my son?"

But as Esau wept, his father did bless his favorite son. It was not the blessing of the firstborn, but it was all Isaac could give. Esau left his father, full of anger, vowing to kill Jacob.

"Run!" Rebekah told Jacob. "Go to my brother Laban and hide. When your brother's anger has eased, you can come back. Go!" And so Jacob ran far away, to wait for Esau to forget.

Esau cried out when he learned that Isaac had given his blessing to Jacob.

Afraid of Esau's anger, Jacob ran away.

בְּרֵאשִׁית כח
Genesis 28

Jacob's Ladder

After the sun had set on the first day of Jacob's travels, he stopped to rest for the night. Lying on the ground with a stone for a pillow, he quickly fell asleep. And he had a dream, a most wonderful dream.

He dreamed of a stairway that started on the ground and reached up to the sky. Angels were going up and down the stairs. And God Himself was standing beside Jacob, and He said, "I give this ground to you and to your children. You shall have many sons and they shall have many sons, and they will spread to the east and the west, to the north and the south. But wherever they go, I will be with them. I will protect them and bring them back to this land. I will not leave you."

Jacob awoke. "The Lord is here, and I did not even know it!" he cried. "This is God's home, and the ladder is the gateway to Heaven." Pouring oil over the stone, he vowed, "If God remains with me, if He protects me on my journey, then the Lord shall be my God. And this stone will mark the place where He dwells."

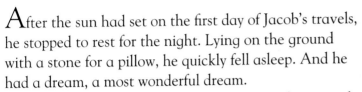

He dreamed of a stairway reaching like a ladder to Heaven.

AND HE DREAMED, AND BEHOLD A LADDER SET UP ON THE EARTH, AND THE TOP OF IT REACHED TO HEAVEN; AND BEHOLD THE ANGELS OF GOD ASCENDING AND DESCENDING ON IT.
GENESIS 28:12

Using a stone for a pillow, Jacob fell asleep.

Jacob and Rachel

Jacob

Rachel

Jacob watched the pretty girl walk to the well.

Shepherdess
Rachel was a shepherdess. She watched over her flocks with care, protecting them from harm.

After traveling for many days, Jacob stopped to drink at a well. Sheep crowded around the well, waiting to drink, for the shepherds in that town gathered all the flocks together in one place before they watered the animals. The well was covered with a huge stone, to keep the water clean, and it took many men working together to move the heavy cover. Because of this, all the shepherds came by the well at the same time, shouting and talking, joking and laughing, as dozens of thirsty sheep jostled and baaed. Jacob pushed into the big, busy crowd of animals and their keepers, and he had to shout when he asked the herdsmen if they knew his uncle, Laban.

"Yes, we know him well," said the shepherds over the din. "And look, here comes his daughter Rachel, bringing his flock."

Jacob turned and saw Rachel for the first time. She was so beautiful! He jumped up and ran to help her—and all by himself he lifted the mighty stone covering the well. Then he kissed Rachel. Weeping, he told her that he was of her family, the son of Rebekah.

Laban himself came out to greet his newfound nephew and to welcome him into the home he shared with Rachel and Leah, his older daughter, just as he had welcomed Abraham's faithful servant so many years before. While Jacob watched lovely Rachel's every movement, Leah watched Jacob with soft, tender eyes.

At last Jacob told the story of how he had come to them, and Laban nodded thoughtfully, saying, "Truly you are my own kinsman."

So Jacob stayed with the little family, helping with the sheep and

Jacob's kiss
When Jacob first realized that Rachel was his cousin, he gave her a kiss. This painting, by artist William Dyce, captures that moment.

After Rachel told him that Jacob had come, Laban came out to greet his kinsman.

Rachel and Leah waited to welcome Jacob.

the goats and the crops. He worked hard, and as he worked he grew to love Rachel more and more, both for her kind ways and for her great beauty. After a month had gone by, Laban said to Jacob, "Is it right that you should work for me and receive no pay? Tell me, what should your wages be?"

"I love Rachel," said Jacob. "I will work for you for seven years if only you will let us wed." And Laban agreed to accept seven years of Jacob's work in exchange for Rachel's hand.

Rachel's beauty
Rachel was so beautiful that Jacob loved her at once. Perhaps she looked like this pretty girl.

Jacob's Wedding

For seven long years Jacob worked hard for his uncle, tending the sheep and helping with the farming. But he loved Rachel so much that the years seemed like just a moment to him. When the time had passed, he said, "Now, Uncle, it is time for Rachel and I to wed."

So Laban made a huge feast and everyone came to celebrate the wedding of Jacob and Rachel. Jacob was happy, and all the

AND JACOB SERVED SEVEN
YEARS FOR RACHEL; AND
THEY SEEMED UNTO HIM
BUT A FEW DAYS, FOR THE
LOVE HE HAD TO HER.
GENESIS 29:20

Laban

Laban gave a feast to celebrate his daughter's wedding.

Here comes the bride
On her wedding day, Rachel (or Leah) would have worn a heavy veil like this. Today the groom looks at his bride, then draws down her veil just before the wedding.

guests were happy for them as they were married, Jacob in his finest clothes, Rachel wearing a beautiful veil.

But in the light of the morning—oh, no! Jacob discovered that he had married not Rachel, but Leah! "What have you done to me?" Jacob demanded of Laban. "I worked for you to marry Rachel! Why did you trick me?"

"In our family, we do not marry off the younger sister before the older one," said Laban stiffly. "In a week's time, I will give you Rachel to be your wife, too, but in exchange, you will have to work for me for another seven years."

Jacob was furious, but he agreed. And so he married Rachel, too, and he loved her very much. But he was bound to work for her father for seven long years more.

Poor Leah. God saw that she was unloved, and so He gave her children to love her, four healthy sons. The years passed and Rachel was envious of Leah, for she still did not have children. She gave her maidservant to Jacob, so that she would have children to raise as her own, and her maidservant had two sons. Now Leah was envious, for she thought that she could have no more children—so she gave her maidservant to Jacob, and the maidservant bore him two more sons. And then Leah did have two more sons with Jacob, after all.

So many sons, and none for Rachel. At last God took pity on her, and she had a baby, little Joseph, Jacob's eleventh son, and his favorite by far. In time Jacob had twelve sons: Reuben and Simeon,

Wedding feast
The Bible says that the wedding feast of Jacob and Leah lasted for one week. During this time family and friends would have gathered to sing, dance, and play music, as in this modern–day village wedding in Iran.

Jacob was angry that Laban had tricked him.

Laban

Jacob

Leah

Jacob married Rachel, too.

Levi and Judah, then Dan and Naphtali, then Gad and Asher, then Issachar and Zebulun, and then Joseph, and then long afterward, Benjamin who was Rachel's son, too. From these sprang the twelve tribes of Israel, each tribe named after one of Jacob's many children.

Leah had many children, but Rachel was childless for many years.

Leah

Rachel

Jacob's Journey Home

Jacob and his family journeyed to Canaan.

By the riverbank, Jacob wrestled with a stranger.

Jabbok River
Jacob sent his family across the Jabbok River, and he camped by the riverbank. The fast-flowing Jabbok feeds into the Jordan River.

Laban and Jacob were alike in one way: they were both tricky. Just as Laban had tricked Jacob at the wedding, Jacob tricked Laban by managing the family's sheep and goats so that his own flocks became larger and larger. But Laban had tried to trick Jacob first, so that he would gain the larger flocks.

Years went by. Then God said to Jacob, "Return to the land of your fathers, and I will be with you." Jacob called Rachel and Leah and his many sons, and on a long caravan of camels, the family set out. Running from Laban's anger, returning to face Esau's anger,

Jacob prayed to God and asked for His help.

As the caravan drew near Jacob's old home, he chose the finest of his flocks and sent them ahead as gifts for Esau. Then he helped his wives and his children and the camels and the sheep to ford a river. While they waited for him on the other side, darkness fell, and so Jacob could not cross. The night was quiet, and Jacob thought about his life and his past, all the things he had done and had not done.

Out of the darkness a stranger appeared, and he demanded that Jacob wrestle him. They wrestled, shoulder against shoulder, all through the night. Jacob twisted his hip, but he fought on.

Esau meets Jacob
The emotions of the brothers' reunion is captured in this engraving by artist Gustave Doré.

Jacob and Esau were reunited at last.

At last the stranger said, "Let me go, for dawn is breaking."

"I will not let you go unless you bless me," said Jacob, panting with pain and exhaustion.

"What is your name?" the man asked.

"Jacob."

"It will be Jacob no more. From this moment, you shall be called Israel," the stranger said. "All who hear it will know that you have struggled with God and with men, and you have prevailed." Then he disappeared, gone as suddenly as he had come.

Looking up, Jacob saw Esau coming, leading his men. Rejoicing, but afraid, he went to his brother, slowly, bowing low seven times as he approached, and Esau ran to greet him. Weeping, they embraced.

"My brother, seeing you is like seeing the face of God," said Jacob. And so the twenty long years apart were gone in a moment.

AND HE HIMSELF PASSED OVER BEFORE THEM, AND BOWED HIMSELF TO THE GROUND SEVEN TIMES, UNTIL HE CAME NEAR TO HIS BROTHER. AND ESAU RAN TO MEET HIM, AND EMBRACED HIM, AND FELL ON HIS NECK, AND KISSED HIM; AND THEY WEPT.
GENESIS 33:3–4

Joseph's Dreams

saffron

cochineal

pomegranate

mollusk shell

kermes insect

Natural dyes
Joseph's coat may have been embroidered, or it might have been dyed with colors like these. Orange came from saffron, pink from cochineal, blue from pomegranate rinds, purple from mollusk shells, and red from kermes insects.

Jacob had twelve sons, but Joseph was his favorite. He gave Joseph a wonderful present: an embroidered jacket, a coat of many colors. When his brothers saw the beautiful coat, it was clear to them once and for all that Jacob loved Joseph more than any of his other sons. So the brothers hated Joseph, so much that they could hardly speak to him.

They hated Joseph even more when he told them about a dream he had had. "We were working in the fields, binding sheaves of wheat," Joseph said. "Suddenly, my sheaf stood up straight and tall. The sheaves that you had made bowed low to it."

"Does that mean you will rule over us?" asked his brothers. Joseph did not answer, but soon he had another dream.

"I dreamed that the Sun, the Moon, and eleven stars were bowing down to me," said Joseph. The brothers were very displeased by this new dream, which seemed to mean the same as the first one. Joseph told Jacob about his latest dream, and even Jacob was worried.

Joseph told his brothers his dreams.

Jacob gave Joseph a beautiful coat.

"Does this mean that we, your mother and your brothers and I, are to bow low before you?" Joseph did not answer, but the meaning of the dreams was clear to everyone.

The days passed, and Joseph's brothers had time to become really angry at him. One day they were out in the fields tending Jacob's flock, and Joseph was sent to meet them.

They saw their brother coming from a long way away. And in the time it took him to get close to them, they hatched a plan to kill him. "Let's throw him into this pit and say that a savage beast ate him!" one said. When Joseph arrived, they tore off his beautiful coat and threw him into the pit. Then, tired from their herding and their plotting, they sat down to rest.

Across the plains came a camel caravan of Ishmaelite merchants. Judah had an idea. "What do we gain by killing Joseph? Let's sell him to the merchants!" The Ishmaelites were happy to get such a fine, strong slave, and for only twenty pieces of silver, too. They took him on to Egypt.

To hide what they had done, Joseph's brothers took his beautiful coat and dipped it in the blood of a goat. Seeing the bloody coat, Jacob was certain that Joseph was dead. "My son! My son!" he wept. "He has been killed by a wild beast!" He mourned his lost son for many days.

balm

cinnamon

fennel seeds

black peppercorns

myrrh oil

myrrh resin

Ishmaelite goods
Traders carried goods such as these from Arabia to Egypt. Cinnamon was used as a spice and a perfume, balm and fennel were used in medicine, myrrh resin and oil for anointing and embalming bodies.

The brothers threw Joseph into the pit.

A band of Ishmaelites came by on their way to Egypt.

The brothers sold Joseph into slavery.

Joseph's coat

Joseph the Slave

Jacob was mourning his son, but Joseph was not dead. When they got to Egypt, the merchants sold him to Potiphar, chief steward to the pharaoh himself. Potiphar liked Joseph, and put him in charge of his household. Because God was with Joseph, Potiphar's home ran very smoothly.

But soon Potiphar's wife noticed Joseph, how strong and handsome he was. Joseph tried to stay out of her way as much as he could, but

*The Ishmaelites sold
Joseph to Potiphar.*

Potiphar

Joseph

But Potiphar's wife liked Joseph a little too much.

one day she took hold of his clothing and held him tight. Very tight. Joseph was shocked at what she whispered in his ear. He struggled and ran away...leaving his torn garment in her hand.

When Potiphar came home, his wife was still upset because Joseph had refused her, and so she showed her husband the torn garment and told terrible lies about Joseph. Potiphar was angry, and suddenly Joseph found himself in prison.

But even in jail, Joseph was not alone. God was with him. And when the cupbearer and the baker to the pharaoh of Egypt himself were sent to the prison for angering the pharaoh, Joseph was there to interpret the strange dreams that the men had.

"In my dream," said the cupbearer, "a grapevine grew so fast that

Women in Egypt
In ancient Egypt, women could own property separate from their husbands. Potiphar's wife, like this regal woman, would have managed her own possessions.

flowers bloomed and fruit ripened before my eyes. I pressed the grapes into Pharaoh's cup, and I gave the cup of wine to him."

"Your dream means that Pharaoh will pardon you," said Joseph. "Soon you will be serving him again, just as you did before. Please, when you see him, ask him to free me."

The baker stepped up. "In my dream," he said, "I had baskets of bread balanced on my head. Birds were eating the bread from the baskets."

Wall painting
The houses of officials, such as Potiphar, would have been decorated with brightly colored wall paintings like this detail of a hunting scene. Raw materials, such as carbon for black and copper for green, were used as paints.

Because of his wife's story, Potiphar had Joseph arrested and sent to prison.

cupbearer Joseph baker

Joseph told the baker and the cupbearer the meaning of their dreams.

Cupbearer
This limestone relief shows a cupbearer serving an Egyptian princess. The pharaoh's cupbearer was a high-ranking official who held an important position of trust. His main duty was to taste food and drink before it was served, to check for poison.

"My friend," Joseph said sadly. "Your dream means that Pharaoh will not forgive you. Soon he will have you killed."

It happened just as Joseph had said. The cupbearer was welcomed back into the pharaoh's house once more, and the baker was put to death. Forgotten by the cupbearer—and the whole world, it seemed—Joseph remained in prison, wondering where God would send him next, and when.

Pharaoh's Dreams

Pharaoh's throne
The pharaoh would have had a special throne for religious ceremonies. It is thought that this gold-plated throne, found in Tutankhamen's tomb in Egypt, was used for such occasions.

Pharaoh had a dream. He dreamed that he was standing by the Nile, when out of the river came seven cows, plump and strong, and they grazed beside the water. But then seven other cows came up, thin and weak, and they devoured the plump cows.

What a strange dream! Pharaoh was wide awake, wondering. Then slowly he fell asleep again, and this time he dreamed that seven ears of grain, full and healthy, grew on a single stalk. But then seven more ears sprouted, poor and dry. The thin ears swallowed the healthy ears right up. Then Pharaoh awoke again.

What could these dreams mean? The next morning, he summoned all the wise men of the land, but none of them could tell him the meaning of his dreams. Finally Pharaoh's cupbearer spoke up. "Sir, when I had offended you...when I was in prison...I had a dream myself. The baker was in prison with me, and he also had a dream. We could not tell what our

Joseph was taken from prison to tell Pharaoh the meaning of his dreams.

Joseph

Impressed, Pharaoh made Joseph an important official.

dreams meant, but a boy there interpreted them for us, and as he told us, it came to pass."

Pharaoh sent for Joseph immediately. He said, "I have heard it said that for you to hear a dream is to tell its meaning."

"Not I, but God," said Joseph.

"Then let God tell you the meaning of my dreams," said Pharaoh. And he told Joseph about his mysterious dreams, and Joseph listened closely.

"God has told you what He is about to do," Joseph told Pharaoh. "The next seven years will be great ones for Egypt, with food for all. After then will come seven years of famine. We must prepare for this time of suffering."

Pharaoh said to everyone there, "Could we find another man like him, a man filled with the spirit of God?" And he put Joseph in charge of the planning for the lean years, and raised him up almost as high as the Pharaoh himself.

As Joseph had foretold, seven good years were followed by seven lean years. And with his careful planning and the help of God, Egypt and its people were saved.

AND PHARAOH SAID UNTO JOSEPH, "GOD HAS SHOWN YOU ALL THIS; THERE IS NONE SO DISCREET AND WISE AS YOU. YOU SHALL BE OVER MY HOUSE, AND ACCORDING TO YOUR WORD SHALL ALL MY PEOPLE BE RULED; ONLY IN THE THRONE WILL I BE GREATER THAN YOU."
GENESIS 41:39–40

Chariot
Egyptian chariots were driven by royalty as well as warriors and hunters. When Joseph became a leader, he also received a chariot to show how important he was.

Joseph

Joseph had workers gather and store grain for the hard years ahead.

Joseph the Leader

Joseph

Simeon was taken prisoner.

The brothers kneeled down before Joseph.

Famine
This statue of a man with a begging bowl was found in Egypt and dates from around 2000 BCE. It shows the suffering of ordinary people during times of famine, a constant threat in the ancient world. The famine in Egypt would have been caused by a drop in the water level of the Nile. The river normally provided the Egyptians with plenty of water for their crops.

AND HE TURNED HIMSELF ABOUT FROM THEM, AND WEPT; AND HE RETURNED TO THEM, AND SPOKE TO THEM, AND TOOK SIMEON FROM AMONG THEM, AND BOUND HIM BEFORE THEIR EYES.
GENESIS 42:24

The famine had spread even to Canaan, where Joseph's brothers and his father were starving. "I hear that there is food in Egypt," said Jacob to his sons. "Go and buy food there. Save our lives!" So ten of Joseph's brothers set out, and only young Benjamin stayed behind with their father, who feared he might meet with disaster.

In Egypt, the brothers went to see the grand vizier, the man in charge of giving what food there was to the poor and the needy. They bowed low before the vizier, and they did not even realize that he was Joseph, their own brother. But Joseph knew them.

They started to explain their errand, but Joseph interrupted. "You are spies, here to discover our secrets!" Joseph said, in the language of the Egyptians. Another man told the brothers what he had said—for though Joseph still remembered Hebrew well, he did not want his brothers to know that he understood them.

"No, no," they said. "We are all brothers, twelve sons of a man in Canaan. But our youngest brother stayed home with our father, and one is no more."

"Spies!" cried Joseph. "You are spies, sent by Egypt's enemies!

Joseph had his brothers' sacks filled with wheat, and their silver secretly put back into the bags.

On the journey home, they discovered the silver.

If you are not spies, prove it by bringing this youngest brother before me." He took the money they had brought to pay for food, and he said, "I will keep one of you as my prisoner. The others may go and fetch this youngest brother, to prove that your words are true and that you are not spies."

The brothers argued among themselves. One said, "How could this happen? We wanted only to buy food!"

But another said, "We are being punished because of what we did to Joseph so long ago."

Then Reuben spoke up. "I told you not to harm him, but you did not listen to me. This is the reckoning!"

Joseph heard all they said. Then he took Simeon from among them and had him bound. Joseph's servants filled the brothers' sacks with grain, and with heavy hearts, the men set off for Canaan.

As they journeyed, they opened the sacks, and found not only food but their money, restored to them. "What does this mean?" they wondered. When at last they returned to their father, they told him what the grand vizier had said, and how the man had kept Simeon and demanded Benjamin.

"It is always me who suffers," said Jacob, an old man now. "First Joseph is killed, then Simeon is captured. And now you would take Benjamin from me."

"I will take care of him," said Judah.

"See that you do," said Jacob mournfully. "If anything happens to him, you will see my white head bent down in grief." And so the brothers set off once more, with rich gifts for the grand vizier, and, this time, with their brother Benjamin.

Recording a harvest
In Egypt, grain was stored in large warehouses. Clerks kept careful records, as shown in this wall painting. Joseph was a good organizer, and he would have been able to provide his brothers with wheat from his supply.

Pieces of silver
In the days before coins, silver was often used as money. Joseph's brothers would have paid for their grain with pieces of silver weighed out on scales.

Benjamin and Joseph

Wine funnel
The brothers drank and were merry at Joseph's meal. Winemaking was common in Egypt. Special funnels like this were used to strain sediment from the wine.

Egyptian foods
Ancient Egyptians usually ate well, and Joseph was a respected leader with plenty of food. The meal he served might have included duck, cucumbers, leeks, onions, garlic, and olives, followed by treats like pomegranates, dates, figs, walnuts, almonds, and wild honey.

As his brothers ate, Joseph wept.

Joseph saw his brothers coming, with Benjamin among them. He sent his servant to fetch them, and they were frightened, thinking that they were going to be arrested. "We were here once before, to buy food," they told him. "As we were traveling home, we opened the bags of grain and found our silver inside. There must have been a mistake; we have brought it back."

"Your God must have returned it to you," the servant said. And he brought Simeon to them, and made them comfortable.

When Joseph arrived, he asked, "How is your aged father? Is he still in good health?"

"He is well," they answered, amazed at his concern.

"And is this your youngest brother?" he said, gesturing to Benjamin. "May God be gracious to you, my boy." Then, with tears springing to his eyes, he hurried out of the room, overcome. When he reappeared, it was time for the meal. The brothers were seated in order of age, from oldest to youngest. "How did he know?" murmured one to another. All received food and drink, but Benjamin was offered by far the most.

Meanwhile, Joseph's servant was following his master's orders: he was filling the bags of the brothers, as before, with grain and returning their silver. And into Benjamin's bag he placed a small silver cup.

The next morning, the brothers set off for home. But they had not

The silver cup was found in Benjamin's sack.

Steward

Benjamin

Silver cups
These cups date from about the same time as the story of Joseph and his brothers. They are about 4,000 years old. The theft of a silver cup would have been a very serious matter—silver was a great luxury, imported into Egypt from Syria. The fact that the cup belonged to Joseph, an important leader, second only to Pharaoh, would have made the punishment even greater.

gone far before the servant rode up behind them and cried, "Thieves! You have taken my master's cup!"

The brothers were stunned, but they opened up their bags to show him that they did not have the cup. From Reuben on down, they opened their bags. No cup, no cup, no cup…finally it was Benjamin's turn. He untied his bag—and took out a small silver cup. The brothers despaired, for this meant that Benjamin, as a thief, would become the slave of the man he had stolen from.

Back in the city, they pleaded with Joseph to release Benjamin. Judah spoke: "Sir, our youngest brother is the special favorite of our father. If Benjamin does not return, sir, our father will surely die of sorrow. We have pledged to return him safely. Take me as your slave in his place."

Then Joseph knew for certain that his brothers had grown into fine men, loving, kind, and good. And he told them, "I am your brother Joseph, whom you sold into Egypt."

The brothers cried out in amazement. "No, do not reproach yourselves," said Joseph. "It was to save lives, your lives, that God sent me ahead of you." Then the brothers, all of them, clung together and wept, with sorrow at the years apart, and with joy at the years ahead.

THEN THEY HASTENED, AND TOOK DOWN EVERY MAN HIS SACK TO THE GROUND, AND OPENED EVERY MAN HIS SACK. AND HE SEARCHED, BEGINNING AT THE ELDEST, AND LEAVING OFF AT THE YOUNGEST; AND THE GOBLET WAS FOUND IN BENJAMIN'S SACK.
GENESIS 44:11–12

Life in Egypt

ax   bow   lyre   women in woolen garments   donkey   men in woolen garments

When Joseph saved his family from the famine, he gave them land in the northern part of Egypt. This area, called Goshen in the Bible, is along the eastern edge of the Nile Delta. It is good pasture land—perfect for Jacob's shepherd sons. The pharaoh of Joseph's time welcomed Joseph's family to his country, and for about a hundred years, the Israelites in Egypt were treated well.

Packing light
In this picture, travelers from the land of Canaan enter Egypt with all of their possessions. This wall painting was found in an Egyptian tomb at Beni-Hasan.

The number of Israelites grew and grew during this time. Tradition says that Jacob's family of seventy people grew to a huge population, becoming a small nation filling the land of Goshen.

Over time, and as the number of Israelites increased rapidly, the Egyptian leaders became

On the Nile
The Nile is Egypt's great river. Many crops are watered by the river, and most of the people live along its banks.

fearful because there were so many of them. Around 1500 BCE., the Israelites were enslaved, and they were forced to make mud bricks, to build houses and roads and even cities—Ramses and Pithom. (They didn't build the pyramids, though. Those were old long before the Israelites became slaves.) Exodus, the part of the Bible that tells the story of God freeing His people from slavery, talks about the sun-baked bricks that the Israelites were forced to make.

By the time Moses was born, life in Egypt had reached a low point for the Israelites.

The Egyptian Pharaoh lived in great luxury, in a palace built with slave labor.

The Egyptians treated their Israelite slaves harshly.

Not only were they forced to work as slaves, but the pharaoh was trying to control the population by killing off the newborn Hebrew baby boys. Moses' mother saved him, by tucking him into a basket made of reeds and putting the basket among the

bulrushes in the Nile River. The daughter of the pharaoh, bathing in the river, spied the basket and took pity on the tiny baby.

By taking in the baby Moses—a baby she knew was a Hebrew baby—and raising him as a member of her family, the pharaoh's daughter gave the Jews their greatest leader. What told her to save this child? It could only be God's plan.

The Exodus
No one knows exactly what route the Israelites, led by Moses, took when they left Egypt. But they probably avoided the most direct route along the Mediterranean coast, where they might have encountered Philistines.

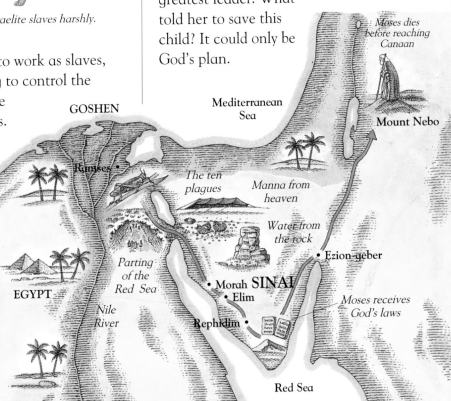

GOSHEN

Mediterranean Sea

Moses dies before reaching Canaan

Mount Nebo

Ramses

The ten plagues

Manna from heaven

Water from the rock

Ezion-geber

Parting of the Red Sea

Morah SINAI

Elim

EGYPT

Nile River

Rephidim

Moses receives God's laws

Red Sea

Moses in the Bulrushes

A new pharaoh came to power, and he saw that the Israelites had grown so numerous that he feared that they would someday overpower the Egyptians. Trying to weaken them, he forced them to become his slaves, working endlessly with mortar and brick, in homes and in the fields.

But still the Israelites multiplied. And then Pharaoh spoke to the Hebrew midwives. "When you deliver an Israelite baby," he said, "if it is a boy, kill him." The midwives were horrified, and they feared God's anger, so they did not do as Pharaoh had told them. Instead, they let all the babies live, and they told Pharaoh, "The Israelite women are so strong, they have their babies without midwives!" More and more babies were born, because God was helping His people to multiply.

Pharaoh declared that any male child born to an Israelite should be put to death.

But Pharaoh was still determined to destroy the Israelites. He made a new law: all boy babies born to an Israelite must be drowned at once.

During this dangerous time, an Israelite woman had a baby boy. She loved him very much, but every day she kept him meant greater danger to her family. So with one last kiss, she put her little one in a basket carefully sealed to keep out water. Then she pushed the basket out into the bulrushes along the Nile. Her daughter, Miriam, hid nearby to watch over the baby.

Soon the daughter of the pharaoh himself, with her handmaidens, came to the river to bathe. Spying the basket tucked in the bulrushes, the pharaoh's daughter pulled it out and was surprised to find a baby boy, crying and crying. "This must be a Hebrew child," she murmured, charmed by the tiny infant.

Miriam appeared by her side. "Could I help you, miss?" she asked. "The baby must be hungry. Shall I find a Hebrew woman to care for the child?"

Pharaoh's daughter looked at Miriam thoughtfully. What good timing! How had this girl happened to be so close by? After a

Golden fishes
These lucky charms may have been worn to protect against accidents on the Nile River. Made of gold, the fish were probably worn by children as hair ornaments.

Basket
This Egyptian basket and lid dates from 1400 BCE. Baskets were used as containers for clothes and food in many households. Moses' mother would have found it easy to make one out of papyrus reeds.

moment, she answered, "Yes, thank you."

So Pharaoh's daughter hired the baby's own mother to care for him. "What will you call this child?" his mother asked. She did not dare look into Pharaoh's daughter's eyes, for fear that she would see the truth.

"I will call him Moses," said Pharaoh's daughter. "And with your help, I will raise him as my own." So Moses' mother lifted up the baby, and she carried him toward his new life.

Keeping cool
Fans made from ostrich feathers were used by servants, known as fan-bearers, in the Egyptian royal court. This ivory-handled fan dates from the time of Moses (about 1300 BCE). Ostriches were a common sight throughout the desert lands of Sinai and Israel in biblical times.

So an Israelite woman hid her baby among the bulrushes on the banks of the Nile.

Servants

Miriam

AND SHE OPENED IT, AND SAW IT, EVEN THE CHILD; AND BEHOLD A BOY THAT WEPT. AND SHE HAD COMPASSION ON HIM, AND SAID, "THIS IS ONE OF THE HEBREWS' CHILDREN."
EXODUS 2:6

Pharaoh's daughter found the baby as his sister watched.

Pharah's daughter

Baby Moses

Servant girl

The Burning Bush

Moses was raised in the pharaoh's own household, yet as a young man he felt like a stranger walking among the Egyptians. On the street one day he saw an Egyptian man beating an Israelite, and he got so angry that he struck the Egyptian man—and killed him. Soon everyone knew what Moses had done, and the pharaoh wanted him put to death.

So Moses fled to the land of Midian, where he rested by a well. A family of seven daughters came to draw water, but shepherds drove them away. Moses defended the women and then watered their flock himself. When the girls' father learned of Moses' kindness, he asked him to stay with the family. Moses did, and he fell in love with one of the daughters, Zipporah. He married her and they made a home together.

Moses killed an Egyptian for beating an Israelite.

AND MOSES SAID UNTO THE LORD, "O LORD, I AM NOT A MAN OF WORDS, NEITHER HERETOFORE, NOR SINCE YOU HAVE SPOKEN UNTO YOUR SERVANT, FOR I AM SLOW OF SPEECH."
GENESIS 4:10

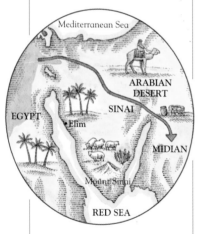

Moses' flight
Moses fled across the harsh Sinai Desert before reaching Midian. There, on Mount Horeb, God appeared out of a burning bush. Later, Moses would receive Gods laws on Horeb, also known as Mount Sinai.

Moses defended seven sisters at the well.

He drove the shepherds away so that the sisters could get water.

Many years passed, and the old pharaoh died. The Israelites, Moses' people, cried out in their bondage, and their cries rose up to God. Hearing them, God remembered eveything He had promised to Abraham. He looked upon the Israelites, and He saw how they suffered. He knew the time had come to save Abraham's offspring, numerous as the stars in the sky.

That day on Horeb, the mountain of God, a blazing fire suddenly burst from a bush. Moses, tending his family's flocks, was amazed to see that the bush was aflame, the flames leaping higher and higher, and yet it was not consumed in the fire. It burned on and on. "I must look closer," thought Moses. As he drew near, God called to him from the burning bush.

"Moses!" cried God. "I am the God of your father, the God of Abraham." Moses hid his face, for he was afraid to look at God. "I have come to rescue My people and bring them to a land flowing with milk and honey. You shall free My people, the Israelites."

"Who am I that the Egyptians will listen to me?" asked Moses, astonished.

"I will be with you, Moses. Throw your rod upon the ground," ordered God. Moses did, and as soon as it touched the ground, the rod turned into a writhing snake. "Pick it up by the tail," God said. Moses did, and the snake became a rod again.

"Now put your hand to your chest," said God. Moses did as He said, putting his hand inside his garment. When he took it back out, his hand was covered with snowy scales. Then Moses put his hand back into his garment again, and the scales disappeared.

"I will be with you," said God. "These signs will show that I have sent you to save My people."

"God, they will not listen to me," said Moses. "I stammer, I stutter, I am slow of speech."

"Who gives man speech? Who makes him silent or deaf, seeing or blind? Is it not I? Now go, and I will be with you."

"God, please, find someone else to do this work, for I cannot," said Moses, pleading.

"Let your brother Aaron speak for you, then, as you speak for Me," God said, angry now, for who dares to defy God? "But you must do as I tell you, Moses."

A bush burst into flames in front of Moses, and God spoke to him.

AND THE ANGEL OF THE LORD APPEARED UNTO HIM IN A FLAME OF FIRE OUT OF THE MIDST OF A BUSH; AND HE LOOKED, AND, BEHOLD, THE BUSH BURNED WITH FIRE, AND THE BUSH WAS NOT CONSUMED.
EXODUS 3:2

GOD CALLED UNTO HIM OUT OF THE MIDST OF THE BUSH, AND SAID, "MOSES, MOSES." AND HE SAID, "HERE AM I."
EXODUS 3:4

Moses Warns Pharaoh

Pharaoh

Aaron

Moses

Moses and Aaron stood before Pharaoh, asking him to let their people go. But Pharaoh refused.

As God had told them, Moses and Aaron appeared before the new pharaoh. "God, the Lord of Israel, says, 'Let my people go.' Do as He says, or you will be punished," they told him.

"Why should I bow before your God?" roared Pharaoh. "Get out!"

The next day, Pharaoh told the taskmasters to stop giving the Israelite slaves the straw they needed to make bricks. "Let the slaves find the straw on their own," Pharaoh said. "But remember—the same number of bricks must be made each day!"

Now the Israelites had to scrabble to find straw to make the thousands and thousands of bricks demanded each day. They struggled all day in the burning sun, gleaning bits of stubble, then rushing back to the brickworks, but they could not keep up. The taskmasters beat them bloody, crying that they must work harder, faster, and make more bricks, more, more, more.

Sickened, Moses watched. A worker said to him, "Why have you made Pharaoh angry with us? We were better off before you came. Now he will work us to death!"

Moses said to God, "Why did You send me to Pharaoh? I have only brought more suffering to Your people."

"Tell the people that I am the Lord," God told Moses. "Tell them that I have heard their cries, and I have remembered My promise to Abraham, to Isaac, and to Jacob. I will free My people from their bondage."

Moses tried to comfort the workers with God's word, but still they suffered. Pharaoh's men drove them harder than ever before.

Slavery
The Egyptians sometimes treated their slaves well, but as the Israelites grew in number, they dealt with their slaves more harshly. Israelites were forced to build Egyptian homes and temples and to tend crops and animals for long hours in the hot sun. If the slaves did not work hard enough, they were punished.

The Israelites were cruelly beaten by their Egyptian masters.

The staffs carried by Aaron and Pharaoh's magicians turned into snakes.

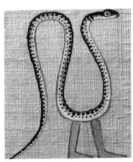

Pharaoh
The powerful rulers of Egypt were called pharaohs. This statue shows Ramses II, who may hav been the pharaoh in the story of Exodus. Ramses II ruled Egypt during the 13th century BCE. The striped headdress symbolizes the pharaoh's high rank.

"Speak to Pharaoh once more," God told Moses. "Ask him to let the Israelites leave Egypt. He will refuse, but I will show him My might, and I will stretch out My hand and free the Israelites."

"But Pharaoh will not listen to me!" cried Moses. "I cannot speak— even the Israelites will not listen to me!"

"Aaron will speak for you. He will be your prophet, as you are mine," said God. "But know this, Moses—Pharaoh's heart will harden against the Israelites, and he will not free them yet. Do not despair. I will free My people. I have promised."

So Moses and Aaron went before Pharaoh again, as God had told them. Pharaoh said, "Produce your marvels. Show me God's power." Aaron threw down his rod and it turned into a snake, just as it had before. Then Pharaoh's magicians threw down their rods, and they turned into snakes, too—but the snake from Aaron's rod ate up all the others. Pharaoh was astounded—but he would not free the Israelites.

Serpent
One of the gods worshiped by the Egyptians was the serpent god, Sito, shown above. When Aaron's serpent ate the Egyptian serpents, it showed God's power over the Egyptian gods.

The Plagues

The first plague: the waters of the Nile turned to blood.

"Pharaoh is stubborn," God said to Moses. "Go to him in the morning, and tell him, 'The Lord has sent me to tell you to let His people go. If you do not free His people, God will send a plague to Egypt.'" Moses did as he was told, but still Pharaoh would not agree to free the people. Moses waved his rod over the water of the Nile, and it turned to blood. The fish died, the river gave off a terrible, sickening smell, and there was no water to drink. Still Pharaoh refused to free the Israelites.

God's second plague was frogs. Hundreds of frogs, thousands of frogs, frogs everywhere, in the streets and in the houses, in the palace, in the pharaoh's bedchamber and his bed, in the ovens and in the bowls where bread was kneaded.

Pharaoh was horrified. "Tell your God to remove the frogs, and I will let His people go," he told Moses and Aaron.

But as soon as the frogs were gone, Pharaoh became stubborn again, and he refused to keep his word.

The second plague: frogs hopped into people's houses.

The third plague was lice, a horrible itching infestation on everyone, every animal and person, in every home and every tent. Still Pharaoh was stubborn.

Then the fourth plague came,

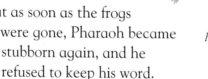

The third plague: lice crawled over every man and woman.

swarms of insects over the land— everywhere except where the Israelites lived. Huge clouds of insects darkened the sky. Their buzzing filled the air. The insects invaded Pharaoh's palace and the Egyptian homes, and they ate the crops standing in the fields and stacked in the storehouses.

Again Pharaoh said he would free the Israelites, if God would only take away the insects. The insects

The fourth plague: a cloud of insects attacked the people.

The fifth plague: the cattle and other livestock were struck by disease.

disappeared, but still Pharaoh would not let the people go.

God's fifth plague was disease among all the livestock of the Egyptians, the cattle, the horses, the mules, the camels, the sheep, the goats. All the animals of the Egyptians died, yet among the animals of the Israelites there was not one death. But Pharaoh would not let the people go. Next God sent a sixth plague, hideous skin diseases that made the Egyptians break out in rashes and painful boils while the Israelites stayed well and whole. But still Pharaoh would not let God's people go.

The sixth plague: people developed horrible skin diseases.

As His seventh plague, God sent hail, thunder, and lightning like fire from the sky. The hail struck down Egyptians and crops, beasts and trees—but the areas where the Israelites lived were untouched. Again, Pharaoh promised to free the Israelites; again, when the thunder and lightning and hail stopped, he would not let the people go. God sent an eighth plague—locusts to eat all the grasses and plants left by the hail. Huge clouds of insects darkened the sky and invaded Pharaoh's palace and all the Egyptian homes, and they ate the crops standing in the fields and stacked in the storehouses.

The seventh plague: hail flattened fields and destroyed crops.

And for the ninth plague, God told Moses to wave his arm toward the sky, and He turned brightest day to blackest night, an endless night that went on and on. But in the homes of the Israelites, there was still light.

The eighth plague: locusts covered the sky and the fields.

Pharaoh summoned Moses. He said, "I will let your people go, but you must leave behind all your livestock."

"No!" cried Moses. "We must keep the livestock so that we will have sacrifices to make before God, to thank him for freeing us from our bondage."

Pharaoh said, "Then be gone from me. I will not free your people." Moses left with a heavy heart, for he knew that God's last plague would be His most terrible.

The ninth plague: an endless night settled over Egypt.

The Tenth Plague

The Israelites marked the doorways of their houses with blood.

In every Egyptian family, the oldest son drew his last breath and died.

Passover feast
At Passover each spring, we celebrate the time when the angel of death passed over the houses of the Israelites. The seder plate is filled with matzoh, charoset, bitter herbs, a shank bone from a lamb, an egg, and saltwater for the tears shed by the slaves long ago.

"I will bring but one more plague upon Egypt," God told Moses. "After that, Pharaoh will let My people go."

Moses warned the people of Egypt, "God says this: toward midnight He will go forth among the Egyptians, and every firstborn son in the land of Egypt shall die. And there shall be a loud cry in all the land of Egypt, such as has never been or will ever be again. But the homes of God's people shall be quiet and safe. And then at last the Pharaoh shall tell God's people to go, to leave this land forever." That was God's last warning, for His last and most terrible plague.

God told the Israelites to sacrifice young lambs and mark their doorways with the animals' blood. "Roast the meat and eat it that same night, quickly, with unleavened bread and with bitter herbs," said God. "And while you eat, be ready to flee. Have your sandals on your feet, your staff in your hands. For that night, I will go through the land of Egypt and strike down every firstborn son, from the son of the pharaoh to the son of the lowest laborer. But when I see the blood, I will pass over the houses of My people."

Then God told them, "This day shall be to you one of remembrance: you shall celebrate it as a festival to the Lord throughout the ages. Seven days you shall eat unleavened bread, and on the first day remove all leavened bread from your homes. This feast marks the day I brought My people out of Egypt. And when your children ask you, 'Why do we do this?' tell them it is to thank the Lord for what He did for you."

AND HE CALLED FOR MOSES AND AARON BY NIGHT AND SAID, "RISE UP, GET YOU FORTH FROM AMONG MY PEOPLE, BOTH YOU AND THE CHILDREN OF ISRAEL; AND GO, SERVE THE LORD, AS YOU HAVE SAID."
EXODUS 12:31

Taking everything they owned with them, the Israelites fled Egypt.

In the middle of the night, when all was quiet and still, God struck down all the firstborn sons in the land of Egypt. Death was everywhere; no Egyptian home was spared. The streets rang and echoed with the wailing. And the pharaoh, grieving for his own firstborn son, called Moses and Aaron to him and said, "Go! Take your people and your flocks, and go and worship your God! Go!"

And so, after more than four hundred years of slavery, the Israelites were free. They ran, gathering up everything they owned and fleeing the land of Egypt, to start new lives in the land that God had promised them.

Saddlebag
When they left Egypt, the Israelites may have carried their possessions in saddlebags much like this one, made of goat hair and wool.

The Parting of the Red Sea

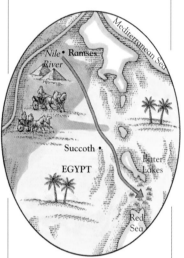

Crossing the sea
The Hebrew words originally translated as "Red Sea" in fact mean "sea of reeds." It is possible that the Israelites crossed over a marshy swamp to the north of the Red Sea.

The Red Sea
The Israelites could have camped at a spot like this by the Red Sea. The sea usually looks blue, but when the algae that grow in the water die, the sea becomes a reddish brown.

So God brought the Israelites out of Egypt. As they traveled, they had only unleavened bread to eat, because when it was time to leave, they had to leave quickly, without waiting for the bread to rise. And God did not lead the people the quickest way to the Promised Land, but in a roundabout way, through the wilderness. A pillar of cloud guided them by day, and a pillar of fire guided them by night, so that they could always see clearly.

But back in Egypt, God had hardened the pharaoh's heart, so that even though the pharaoh had sent the Israelites away, now he wanted to capture them again. Chasing Moses and his followers, the Egyptians caught up with them by the edge of the Red Sea.

The people were very frightened. "Why did you take us out of Egypt only to let us die in the wilderness?" they asked Moses.

But Moses cried, "Have no fear! The Egyptians who you see today, you will never see again. The Lord will do battle for you!"

God said to Moses, "Tell the Israelites to go forward. Then lift up your rod and hold out your arm over the sea, for the Israelites will march on dry ground. The Egyptians will follow them, and then the pharaoh will see My power and glory."

Moses held out his arm over the sea, and God drove back the water so that there was a path of dry ground. The sea was split, and the Israelites went on, men, women, and children, animals and cooking pots, tents and camels, with walls of water to the right and to the left. The Egyptians followed after them, all of the pharaoh's warriors, chariots, and horses. God watched from a pillar of fire and cloud, and soon He locked the wheels of the chariots so that they moved slowly, so slowly. The Israelites pulled farther and farther ahead.

Then God told Moses once more, "Hold out your arm over the sea." And he did, and the waters of the sea came rushing back. The Israelites were safe on dry ground, but the Egyptians were trapped, and their heavy armor held them down so that every one drowned. And so God delivered the Israelites from Egypt on that day.

With timbrels and music, Moses and Aaron led the Israelites in rejoicing. "In Your love You lead the people You redeemed," they sang. And Miriam, their sister, played her timbrel like thunder and told the people, "Sing to the Lord, for He has triumphed gloriously!"

שְׁמוֹת יג–טו

As the waters parted, Moses led
his people across the Red Sea.

Then the water closed over the Egyptians.

God Watches Over the Israelites

God sent flocks of quail to feed the Israelites in the desert.

The Israelites caught the quail and roasted them.

Quail
Migrating quail fly across the Sinai Desert twice a year. Tired from the long flight, they fly low and are easily caught.

Free at last, the people wandered in the desert for many days and nights. They were hungry, they were footsore, and, worst of all, they had no idea where they were going or when they would get there. "Why did God free us from slavery only to let us suffer and die in the desert?" they asked Moses.

God told Moses, "The people will eat. First there will be meat, and then I will rain down bread from the sky, enough to feed the people every day. And on the sixth day there will be a double portion."

Manna
Some scholars think that the manna may have come from the hammada shrub, above, which grows in southern Sinai. When insects feed on its branches, it produces a sweet, white liquid. Today, Bedouin people use it as a sweetener.

In the morning, the ground was covered with sweet manna.

The people were told to gather only as much as they could eat in one day.

The people did not believe Moses when he told them that the sky would rain food... but so it happened. First a flock of quail flew overhead, and everyone ate and ate the roasted meat.

Then in the morning, dew fell, and when it dried, something new was there on the ground. All the people rushed to collect the strange food, like nothing the Israelites had ever tasted before. Manna, they called it, and it was sweet and filling, like wafers soaked in honey. What little manna there was left over at the end of the day spoiled very quickly, so that it could not be eaten.

Each day the manna fell from the sky, but on the sixth day twice as much rained down—the double portion that God had told Moses would come. "God means for us to rest on the Sabbath, the seventh day," Moses told the people. "Save some of this manna for tomorrow; it will not spoil." He was right. There was food for all on the seventh day.

Then, as they traveled on, the Israelites came to a place where there was no water to drink. Again they said to Moses, "Why did God take us out of Egypt, only to let us die in the desert?"

"What shall I do with these people?" Moses asked God. "They are never happy! But it is true that they need water."

"Take the people to Horeb," God said. "And standing before them, strike the stone there with your rod."

And when Moses struck the rock, water poured forth where there had been none before, flowing and bubbling, and all the people drank the fresh, cool water.

Moses struck the stone with his rod, and water gushed out.

"BEHOLD, I WILL STAND BEFORE YOU THERE UPON THE ROCK IN HOREB; AND YOU SHALL SMITE THE ROCK, AND THERE SHALL COME WATER OUT OF IT, THAT THE PEOPLE MAY DRINK." AND MOSES DID SO IN THE SIGHT OF THE ELDERS OF ISRAEL.
EXODUS 17:6

The Ten Commandments

BUT MOSES DREW
NEAR UNTO THE THICK
DARKNESS WHERE
GOD WAS.
EXODUS 20:21

Seven weeks after fleeing Egypt, the Israelites entered the wilderness of Sinai and camped there, in front of the mountain. Moses went up Mount Sinai to speak to God, and God said, "I bore you on eagles' wings and brought you to me. In three days, I will give you the words that will make you My own holy nation. Let My people remain pure during this time."

Moses went down the mountain and told the Israelites what God had said, told them that this was a time for rejoicing. And on the third day, as morning dawned, there was thunder, and lightning, and a dense cloud upon the mountain,

God called Moses to Him, and gave him the Ten Commandments carved on two stone tablets.

and a loud blast of a horn. Moses led the people to the foot of the mountain, and there they waited for God's word. Moses climbed up to speak to God alone. Smoke filled the air, and God called Moses to come nearer to Him, to receive His word.

"I am the Lord your God, who brought you forth out of bondage. You shall have no other gods before Me," God said.

"You shall not make for yourself a sculptured image of any other god," God said.

"You shall not swear falsely by My name," God said.

"Remember the Sabbath day, and keep it holy," God said.

"Honor your father and mother," God said.

"You shall not murder," God said.

"You shall not commit adultery," God said.

"You shall not steal," God said.

"You shall not bear false witness against your neighbor," God said.

"You shall not covet your neighbor's house, or anything that is your neighbor's," God said.

Carrying two stone tablets carved with these ten commandments in God's own hand, Moses went to bring God's word to the Israelites. He was so happy, so filled with the spirit of God—but he was shocked at what he found at the foot of the mountain.

Mount Sinai
Moses received God's laws on Mount Sinai, or Mount Horeb, as it is sometimes called in the Bible. Mount Sinai may be the mountain Jebel Musa, or "Mountain of Moses," one of a group of peaks in the south of the Sinai Peninsula.

The Israelites camped at the foot of Mount Sinai.

The Golden Calf

As they waited for Moses to come back with God's word, the people had become restless. "Maybe Moses will never come back to us," they said. Days went by, though they passed like a moment to Moses.

"Where is he?" asked the people. "He is not coming back to us!" And they called on Aaron to make them a god to worship.

Driven almost insane by their endless demands, Aaron collected all the gold that the people had brought from Egypt and, melting it down, he made a golden calf. The people worshiped the calf as a god, and Aaron built an altar before it so that they could make burnt sacrifices to it.

God was angry—very, very angry. He called to Moses who was traveling down the mountain, "Your people are already defying My commandments! My anger will destroy them!"

"Please, God, spare them!" cried Moses. "Do not let the Egyptians say that You saved Your people only to kill them in the mountains, only to wipe them off the face of the earth! God, spare them!"

Faster and faster, Moses ran down the mountain. Long before he could see them, he heard the people singing. He tore into the camp and he cried out at what he saw there—his own people dancing and praising a false god! In his rage, Moses dashed the sacred stone tablets to the ground. Then he seized the golden calf and ground it into powder, and he forced the people to drink the powder, so that nothing of the terrible sculpted image remained.

"How could you do this?" Moses said to Aaron. "How could you bring such sin upon the people?"

"What could I do? They did not believe that you were coming back," said Aaron.

Moses turned from him and cried, "Whoever is for the Lord, come here!" Some of the people came to him at once, the entire tribe of Levi, and Moses told them to slay brothers, sisters, neighbors, friends—all who did not worship the God of Israel. Three thousand died that day. And at last Moses said to those who remained, "Dedicate yourselves to God today, so that He may bless you always."

Then Moses went before God and said, "God, forgive Your people if You can. And if You cannot, let me disappear from Your records of this time. Let all of us be forgotten together." "Go now," said God. "Lead the people as I told you. But I will remember those who have sinned against me."

Egyptian bull god
Aaron's golden calf could have been based on Apis, an Egyptian bull god depicted in this painting from Thebes in Egypt. Pagan gods were often represented as bulls in ancient times. Bulls were known for their strength and fearlessness and were used as symbols of fertility and power.

AND IT CAME TO PASS, AS SOON AS HE CAME NIGH UNTO THE CAMP, THAT HE SAW THE CALF AND THE DANCING; AND MOSES' ANGER WAXED HOT, AND HE CAST THE TABLES OUT OF HIS HANDS, AND BROKE THEM BENEATH THE MOUNT.
EXODUS 32:19

The people danced
and sang in front of it.

Aaron made a
golden calf for the
people to worship.

Seeing them, Moses
smashed the stone
tablets in fury.

Balaam's Donkey

Making their way through the desert, the Israelites set up camp close to the land of Moab. Their numbers grew and grew until Balak, the Moabite king, sent his advisers to offer a seer great riches to curse the Israelites and drive them away. The seer, Balaam, listened to their offer and said, "I will curse them, if God allows it."

But that night, God told Balaam, "Do not curse My people. They are blessed. Go with these men if you will, but do as I command you."

In the morning, Balaam did go with the men, for the lure of their gold was great. He was riding on his donkey, his companion of many years, when suddenly the animal saw an angel standing in the road, holding a sword. Balaam could not see the angel, and he did not know why his donkey swerved off the road. He beat her to drive her back.

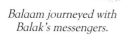

The land of Moab
Balak felt threatened by the Israelites when they camped in the plains of Moab, to the east of the Dead Sea.

Balaam journeyed with Balak's messengers.

THEN THE LORD OPENED THE EYES OF BALAAM, AND HE SAW THE ANGEL OF THE LORD STANDING IN THE WAY, WITH HIS SWORD DRAWN IN HIS HAND; AND HE BOWED HIS HEAD, AND FELL ON HIS FACE.
NUMBERS 22:31

Seeing the angel, Balaam's donkey dropped to the ground.

Again the angel stood in their way. The poor frightened donkey pressed herself against a wall at the side of the road, crushing Balaam's foot. He beat her again.

A third time the angel appeared, in a place so narrow that the donkey could not go to the right or to the left. So she dropped down right where she was. Furious, Balaam beat her.

Then the donkey spoke. "Why are you beating me?" she asked. "Why have you beaten me three times today?

"You have embarrassed me!" cried Balaam. "If I had a sword, I would kill you!"

"We have been together many years," said the donkey. "Have I ever acted this way before?" And then God opened Balaam's eyes so that at last he could see the angel, too.

"Your donkey has saved you," the angel told Balaam. "You may pass, but remember. Speak only the words God puts in your mouth."

When Balaam reached Balak, the two men went together to the

Beast of burden
Donkeys were among the earliest working animals. A donkey could pull a plow, or carry a heavy load, a "burden."

High on a mountaintop, Balaam blessed the Israelites.

Balaam traveled back home.

Balak could not believe that Balaam would not curse the Israelites.

clay bones

model of sheep's liver

mountaintop. Balaam looked out over all the Israelites spread across the land. Then he spoke. "How lovely are your tents, O Jacob, your dwelling places, O Israel," he murmured. "I cannot curse when God has not cursed. These people have been blessed by the Lord. May their fate be mine!"

"What are you saying?" cried Balak. "I hired you to curse them, and you are blessing them!"

"I speak only God's words," said Balaam. And he turned and set out on his journey home.

Tools of the trade
Balaam was a diviner, or fortune teller. In ancient times diviners used objects, such as a clay model of a sheep's liver and animal bones, shown above, to make predictions. The bones were thrown down and the pattern they made was studied to tell the future.

Life in Canaan

Moses led the people faithfully for years and years, and yet he never entered the Promised Land—he only glimpsed it from a mountaintop. What did he see? A land "flowing with milk and honey," the Bible tells us, which means it was rich and green, lush with crops and animals. The Israelites conquered Canaan with God's help, and then, at long last, they were able to settle down in this wonderful new place.

The Israelites were used to living as nomads, setting up camps here and there and moving their livestock from place to place. In Canaan, they built homes, and learned new skills like the peoples around them. They learned how to be farmers, stonemasons, potters, builders, metal workers, and more.

The Canaanites were skilled craftsmen.

When the Israelites arrived, there was conflict with the Canaanites right away. The Canaanites worshiped many gods, including Baal, who is often mentioned in the Bible. (Baal was the chief god of the Canaanites, but the name "Baal" was also used for several different gods represented by idols.) The Israelites, of course, worshiped only one God, and they had no carved images of Him—that was forbidden by the Commandments.

The Promised Land was rich and fertile, "flowing with milk and honey."

Eventually, the Promised Land was divided into areas for each of the twelve tribes descended from the sons of Jacob. There were designated areas for the tribes of Judah, Issachur, and Zebulun, the tribes of Simeon, Reuben, and Gad, the tribe of Benjamin, the tribes of Dan, Asher, and Napthali, and the tribes of Ephraim and Manasseh, the sons of Joseph. The tribe of Levi, the Levites, did not have a special location. Their job was to supervise the worship of God.

At first the Israelites did not have a king—they had judges, or leaders, chosen to make sure that the laws of God were followed. Then, when the people were under attack by the Philistines (a powerful people on the Mediterranean coast of Canaan), the Israelites asked for a king to lead them. Saul became the first king, then David, then David's son Solomon. Later the kingdom was divided into two countries: Israel, in the north, and Judah, in the south. In time, both Israel and Judah were conquered. After the Second Temple was destroyed by the

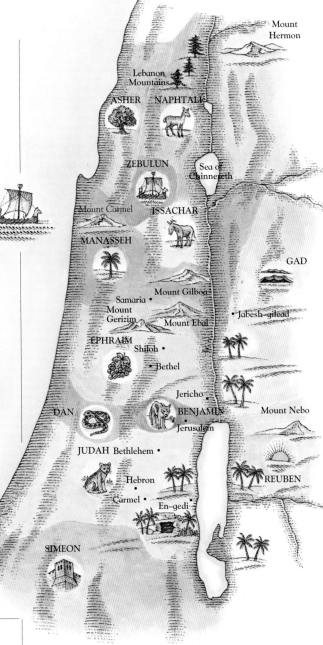

The Promised Land was divided among the twelve tribes descended from Jacob. Each tribe had its own symbol.

Romans, Jews still lived in the area, but they had no true home there until 1948. Then at last, in a modern-day miracle, Israel was reborn once again as the Jewish homeland.

Saul

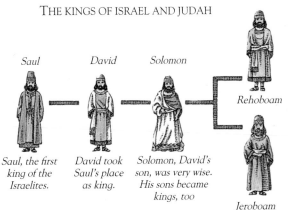

THE KINGS OF ISRAEL AND JUDAH

Saul — *David* — *Solomon* — *Rehoboam*

Jeroboam

Saul, the first king of the Israelites.

David took Saul's place as king.

Solomon, David's son, was very wise. His sons became kings, too

Numbers 13, 14; Deuteronomy 31, 34

The Promised Land

Moses chose twelve men, one from each of the twelve tribes, and he sent them ahead into Canaan, the land God had promised to the Israelites. For forty days the men were gone, scouting the new land. Then Joshua, Caleb, and the others returned, bearing a huge bunch of grapes. "The country is rich, flowing with milk and honey!" they exclaimed. "But the people there are strong, and the cities are well guarded. We will surely lose any battle with them."

Caleb and Joshua still wanted to attack, but the other spies were afraid, and the people became afraid, too. "Why did God free us from Egypt, only to let us die in the wilderness?" they moaned, as they had moaned so many times before. "We cannot fight Canaan! We will be killed!"

Cluster of grapes
The Promised Land was rich and fertile. The first Israelites to see it found bunches of grapes so large that it took two men to carry them!

AND THEY TOLD HIM, AND SAID, "WE CAME UNTO THE LAND WHERE YOU SENT US, AND SURELY IT FLOWS WITH MILK AND HONEY; AND THIS IS THE FRUIT OF IT."
NUMBERS 13:27

The spies returned from Canaan, excited by the rich and fertile land they had seen.

Moses called Joshua and told him that he must lead the people into the Promised Land.

Moses

Joshua

"How long will the people doubt Me?" said God with anger. He had rescued the people from slavery. He had fed them manna in the wilderness. He had given them water in the desert. Yet still they did not trust in His power.

"Forgive them, God," begged Moses.

"I will not destroy them," said God. "But of those who have seen My signs in Egypt and in the wilderness, none will enter the Promised Land. Only Caleb and Joshua, because they alone trusted in Me, will dwell there. For forty years My people will wander, until all who remember slavery are gone."

The Promised Land was gone; it would always be a far-away dream for those who had not believed God's word, even though they had seen His miracles. "We will fight the Canaanites!" the people said then. "God will be with us!"

"It is too late," said Moses sadly. And it was. Forty long years passed, and then, when Moses knew his end was near, he called Joshua to his side. "You must lead our people into the Promised Land," he told him.

"I will be strong," said Joshua, barely able to speak for grief. He helped Moses to the top of the mountain, where Moses looked out over the distant land that he would never know.

Soon, very soon, Moses died, and he was mourned by all. Never before, and never since, has there been another like him.

"FOR YOU SHALL SEE THE LAND AFAR OFF; BUT YOU SHALL NOT GO INTO THE LAND WHICH I GIVE THE CHILDREN OF ISRAEL."
DEUTERONOMY 32:52

Canaan
The valley of Jezreel, shown here, is located in what was once the northern part of Canaan. Though it was known as a nation flowing with milk and honey, Canaan's landscape ranged from green hills to barren desert.

Joshua Is Called by God

Joshua was ready to lead the people into the Promised Land.

God spoke to Joshua. "Moses, My servant, has died," He said. "Now arise, cross the River Jordan, and take My people into the land I have given them, the land of Israel."

Joshua listened to His words. "As I was with Moses, so I will be with you," God told Joshua. "Be strong and of good courage. You are the leader of your people now, Joshua. I will not fail you, or forsake you. Be strong and of good courage, for I am with you wherever you go."

Then Joshua went to the people he led, and he told them to prepare for traveling. "In three days we will cross the Jordan to take the land that God has given us," he said. He warned the mightiest of his men that only when the Promised Land was conquered would they be able to rest.

The men agreed. "Wherever you send us, we will go, if God is with you, as He was with Moses," they said. And like God, they blessed Joshua, saying, "Be strong and of good courage."

"AS I WAS WITH MOSES, SO I WILL BE WITH YOU; I WILL NOT FAIL YOU, NOR FORSAKE YOU."
JOSHUA 1:5

"BE STRONG AND OF GOOD COURAGE; FOR YOU SHALL CAUSE THIS PEOPLE TO INHERIT THE LAND WHICH I SWORE UNTO THEIR FATHERS TO GIVE THEM."
JOSHUA 1:6

The men pledged to follow Joshua, because God was with him.

Rahab Saves the Spies

Right away, Joshua sent two spies into Jericho. The city, built to withstand attack, was surrounded by high walls, so strong and so thick that people lived in homes set right into the stonework. Joshua's spies stayed there with the woman Rahab, who welcomed travelers.

In the dark of night, the king's men pounded on Rahab's door, demanding the spies. She hurried to see what the noise was about. "There were two men here, but they left," Rahab said. "Hurry and you may still catch them!"

While the two spies hid on her roof, Rahab swore to the king's men that they were gone.

As soon as the men were gone, Rahab ran to the roof, where she had hidden the spies under piles of flax. "We have heard of your God's power," she whispered. "When you take the country, remember that I have protected you and spare my family!"

She lowered a crimson rope to the ground so they could escape. "Mark your window with this red cord," the spies said, holding it, "and we will know to protect all who are within your home when the battle comes." Then they disappeared into the darkness.

Rahab helped the spies escape from Jericho.

Flax
Linen is made of flax, a plant with pretty purple flowers. Stems of the flax plant were soaked in water to separate the fibers, then dried on a flat roof like Rahab's. The dry fiber was combed to separate the threads, and at last the threads were woven into linen.

The Battle of Jericho

As the waters parted, the priests carried the Ark of the Covenant across the Jordan River.

The spies returned that night, creeping through the sleeping camp. "The land is ours," they reported to Joshua. "God has given it to us." It was time to take the Promised Land at last. Joshua woke the people and told them to cleanse themselves, for God would soon perform wonders among them. Joshua's men spread the word: "Follow the Ark. It will lead you on a path you have never traveled before."

The next morning, Joshua led the Israelites to the banks of the Jordan River. As they had been told, the people followed the Ark of the Covenant, which was carried by the priests. The sacred box held the stones Moses himself had carved with the Ten Commandments, after he had smashed the ones created by God. "Now march," said Joshua. "And when you reach the river, do not stop."

The Israelites circled the city, shouting to the skies.

The seven priests blew their horns.

"WHEN THEY MAKE A LONG BLAST WITH THE RAM'S HORN, AND WHEN YOU HEAR THE SOUND OF THE HORN, ALL THE PEOPLE SHALL SHOUT WITH A GREAT SHOUT; AND THE WALL OF THE CITY SHALL FALL DOWN FLAT."
JOSHUA 6:5

While the people waited on shore, the Ark bearers walked right into the river—and as they did, the waters of the mighty Jordan stopped flowing and piled up on one side of them. So just as their parents and grandparents had crossed the Red Sea so many years before, the Israelites walked across the dry bed of the Jordan River.

The battle lay ahead. But God would be with them. He had told Joshua how to conquer the city.

Soldiers led the way, followed by seven priests, blowing seven rams' horns. Behind them came the Ark of the Covenant, then the people. More troops brought up the rear of the procession. And for six days in a row the long line of soldiers and priests, trumpeters and Ark and followers of God's word circled the city once each day. On the seventh day, the priests blew a long blast, so long and so powerful that the earth seemed to tremble. "Shout!" cried Joshua. "Shout! God has given you this land! Let Him hear you!"

Then all the people shouted, with hope, with praise, with God's strength, their voices rising up to the sky. The walls of the city began to shake and to shift and then to fall, and the Israelites kept shouting, now with amazement and joy, and they ran into the city, climbing over the broken, crushed walls. Rahab and her family, protected by the crimson cord, were saved, the only ones spared in all of Jericho.

The Israelites had left the wilderness forever, and on that day and ever after they rejoiced in the new life that they had begun, in the land that God had promised to His own people.

Shofar
Joshua's men would have steamed a ram's horn to make it soft, then bent the wide end to make a shofar. Today, we hear the deep, haunting sounds of the shofar during services on the High Holy Days.

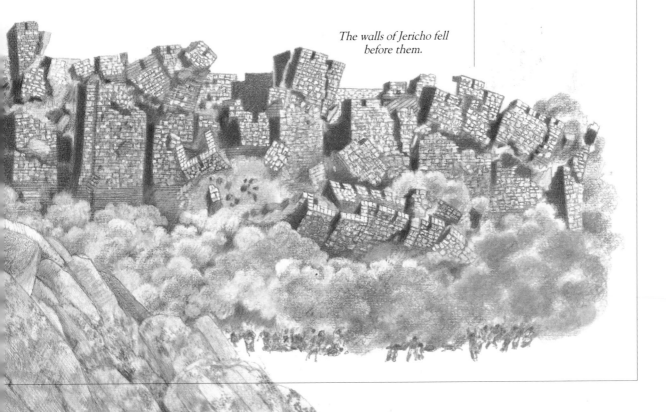

The walls of Jericho fell before them.

Gideon's Call

Time passed, and because the Israelites did not keep their covenant with God He gave them over to the fierce Midianites for seven years.

Near the end of that time, young Gideon looked up from threshing wheat to see an angel of God. "God has chosen you as His messenger," the angel told him. "You will lead an army, and you will defeat the Midianites." Then the angel touched his staff to Gideon's meat and bread. A fire sprang up—and the angel disappeared.

Then God Himself called to him. "Destroy your father's altar to the false gods!" He commanded.

Gideon did—and the next day, filled with the spirit of God, he called for an army to fight the Midianites. From across the countryside, men rallied to his side. There were tall men, small men, thin men, fat men, bold men, shy men, and all wanted to fight for the one true God.

"You have too many men," God told Gideon. "With My help, you will need only a few. Tell the men who fear the battle to return to their homes." After the fearful men left, the army had dwindled from 32,000 men to 10,000 men. Still too many.

"Take them to the river to drink," God told

AND THE ANGEL OF THE LORD APPEARED UNTO HIM, AND SAID UNTO HIM, "THE LORD IS WITH YOU, YOU MIGHTY MAN OF VALOR."
JUDGES 6:12

Gideon smashed the pagan altar.

Gideon took his men to the spring to drink, then chose those who would fight with him.

Gideon. "Divide those men who lap the water from those who kneel." Most of the men drank right from the river. Only three hundred lapped water from their hands—and those men, the few who stayed alert to their surroundings even as they drank, became Gideon's army.

The night before the battle, Gideon stole into the enemy camp and heard one soldier telling another about a dream. The second soldier said, "Your dream can mean only one thing: God is giving this country to the Israelites."

Gideon quickly returned to his own men and wakened them.

"God has given us victory! Come now!" he cried. He gave every man a ram's horn, a jar, and a torch. "Watch me!" he said.

Creeping through the night, the men circled the Midianite camp and formed a circle around it. Just as the night watch changed in the camp, Gideon's army blew their horns and smashed their jars, making a deafening racket. The Midianites scrambled in confusion, and Gideon's men chanted, "A sword for God! A sword for Gideon!" But Gideon's men never lifted a sword. God turned the Midianites' swords one against another. By the morning the country belonged to the Israelites once more.

Spring of Harod
At God's command, Gideon watched to see how his soldiers drank from the waters of this spring. Those who cupped the water in their hands, rather than putting their faces in the water, were chosen to fight. One interpretation is that God chose those who were the most alert and ready for battle.

Gideon's army entered the camp by night.

Samson and the Lion

"An angel of God came to me!" a woman exclaimed to her husband. "He told me that I would have a baby, a son, and that he would be promised to God, and that we should never cut his hair." And soon enough, they were the parents of a boy named Samson. His mighty strength was the wonder of all. It was a gift from God.

At the time Samson was a young man, Israel was ruled by the Philistines. Samson saw a Philistine woman who was a great beauty, and he wanted to marry her. "Why marry a Philistine?" said his parents. "Aren't there plenty of nice young women of our own kind?" But Samson would have no other.

Lion
Lions were the most dangerous animals living in Canaan. They were a constant threat to livestock and to people. Samson tore a lion apart with his bare hands—a feat of incredible strength.

Samson killed a lion, tearing it apart with his bare hands.

So Samson and his parents set out to meet the beautiful woman. One hot afternoon, Samson walked ahead of his parents. Suddenly a mighty lion sprang out and attacked him! Filled with the spirit and strength of God, he seized the lion and tore it to pieces.

When Samson's parents caught up to him, he did not tell them what had happened. They went on, and after he saw the woman, he set a wedding date right away. Samson and his family returned home. Then, a year later, they set out to make the wedding journey to the land of the Philistines.

A year later, Samson found sweet honey in the lion's carcass.

In that whole year, Samson had never told his parents about killing the lion. Once again he walked ahead of his parents, and this time he saw the lion's body lying by the side of the road. Getting closer, he saw that the skeleton was filled with clear honey. A swarm of bees buzzed around Samson as he reached in and scooped up honey for his family to eat as they traveled—but he did not tell his parents where he had found the honey.

The wedding feast was very grand, and as the Philistine guests celebrated, Samson proposed a game. "I have a riddle for you, and you must answer it in seven days' time," he said. "Here it is: out of the eater came forth meat, out of the strong came forth a sweet. Tell me, what have I described?"

No one could guess. Soon some of the wedding guests threatened Samson's wife, demanding, "Tell us the answer to the riddle!" She went to Samson and said, "Samson! There should be no secrets between a man and his wife. Tell me, what is the answer to your riddle?" She wheedled and she whined, and finally Samson told her the answer.

On the seventh day, just as the sun set, the wedding guests answered Samson's riddle: "What is stronger than a lion? What is sweeter than honey?" they said.

"No man alive could have guessed that!" cried Samson. "My wife has tricked me! She has given you the answer!" In a rage, he killed thirty of the men. Then he left, with his father and his mother, and went home, vowing that he would never be betrayed again.

Braided hair
Samson was a Nazarite, a person dedicated to God. Nazarites had to promise never to cut their hair. Samson wore his uncut hair braided, like the prince in the stone sculpture above.

Samson and Delilah

Delilah tied Samson with seven fresh tendons.

She bound Samson with new rope.

She wove his hair into her cloth.

AND DELILAH SAID TO SAMSON, "TELL ME, I PRAY YOU, WHERE YOUR GREAT STRENGTH LIES, AND WHERE YOU MIGHT BE BOUND TO AFFLICT YOU."
JUDGES 16:6

Samson, with his great strength, had stolen the gateposts and the town gate of the Philistines, and they were furious that he had left their city defenseless. So when Samson fell in love with a beautiful woman named Delilah, the Philistine leaders told her, "Coax him and find out what makes him so strong, and how we can overpower him, and we will reward you richly."

Delilah wanted that reward more than she had ever wanted anything. So she began pestering Samson endlessly: "Samson, tell me, what makes you so strong? How could you be made helpless?"

"If I were to be tied up with seven fresh tendons, I should become as weak as an ordinary man," Samson said.

So Delilah tied Samson up with seven fresh tendons, and soon after, the Philistines attacked him. Samson broke through the ties easily and defeated the Philistine men. But Delilah still wanted that reward, and she said, pouting, "Samson! You have lied to me! Tell me, how could you be tied up?"

Weaving
In weaving, threads are intertwined to make cloth. This nomadic woman is weaving on a horizontal loom, similar to the one Delilah would have used.

"If I were to be bound with new ropes that have never been used, I would become as weak as an ordinary man," said Samson.

So Delilah bound Samson with new ropes. But Samson broke right through them as if they were thread. "You have been deceiving me!" said Delilah. "Tell me, how could you be overcome?"

"If you weave seven locks of my hair into your cloth, I will be weak as an ordinary man," he said. Of course, she did weave seven locks of his hair into her cloth while he slept. But when he woke up, Samson simply pulled his hair out of the weaving, strong as ever.

But Delilah nagged and pestered, on and on. "How can you say you love me when you don't confide in me?" she said to Samson. At every turn she asked him for the secret of his great strength—and at last Samson gave in. "No razor has ever touched my head," he told her.

Delilah watched as the Philistines took Samson away to prison.

Philistine headdress
The Philistines lived along the Mediterranean coast in southwest Canaan from 1200 BCE to 600 BCE. They had a well-organized army. The soldiers wore distinctive feathered headdresses, as shown in the stone carving above, which made them appear very tall. They fought with iron swords and spears.

"If my hair were cut, my strength would leave me in an instant."
Delilah could tell that this was the truth at last. She sent for the Philistines and their money. Then she lulled the mighty Samson to sleep in her lap. While he slept, Delilah and the Philistines shaved off his hair, and then, to wake him, Delilah cried, "Samson! The Philistines are upon us!" Samson awoke—and was stunned to find himself drained of his great strength, weak as an ordinary man. The Philistines blinded him. Then they took him away and put him into their prison, and Delilah collected her reward.

AND HE TOLD HER ALL HIS HEART, AND SAID UNTO HER, "THERE HAS NOT COME A RAZOR UPON MY HEAD; FOR I HAVE BEEN A NAZARITE UNTO GOD FROM MY MOTHER'S WOMB; IF I BE SHAVEN, THEN MY STRENGTH WILL GO FROM ME, AND I SHALL BECOME WEAK, AND BE LIKE ANY OTHER MAN."
JUDGES 16:17

Samson Destroys the Temple

Samson pushed against the pillars of the temple.

Months had passed. Samson, his spirit broken, lay in the Philistines' jail, almost forgotten by his captors. The Philistines were making merry at their temple, planning a sacrifice to their god. "Bring Samson here!" one cried. "We can make him dance for us!"

Several men ran to the jail and brought Samson out, marching him through the streets in chains. He was thin and pale. No one noticed that his hair had started to grow back.

At the temple, the Philistines forced him to dance while they laughed at him. Samson paused to catch his breath, and he said to the boy holding his chains, "Let me put my hands on the pillars, just to get my balance. Then I will dance even better." The boy loosened the chains, and Samson stood for a moment with his hands flat against the pillars.

"Please, God," he prayed. "Remember me now." Then, his mighty strength restored by God just for that moment, he pushed with all his might. The Philistines' temple shook, and the Philistines looked up, alarmed. Then the stone pillars and the roof and the walls began to fall, and Samson cried, "Let me die with the Philistines!" The temple crashed down on them, killing everyone.

AND SAMSON CALLED UNTO GOD, AND SAID, "O LORD GOD, REMEMBER ME, I PRAY YOU, AND STRENGTHEN ME, I PRAY YOU, ONLY THIS ONCE, O GOD, THAT I MAY BE THIS ONCE AVENGED OF THE PHILISTINES."
JUDGES 16:28

The temple came crashing down on the Philistines and on Samson.

Ruth and Naomi

Ruth and Naomi journeyed together to Bethlehem, while Orpah returned to Moab.

Orpah

Ruth

Naomi

Boaz watched Ruth working in the field.

Bethlehem
Ruth and Naomi would have traveled for many days before they arrived at Naomi's old home in Bethlehem. The journey would have been a difficult one because Naomi was no longer young and Bethlehem is set high up on a hill.

Naomi and her husband left Israel to escape a terrible famine. They took their two sons and traveled to Moab, where life was easier and food and water were plentiful. But the Moabites did not follow the Israelites' faith, and when her husband died, Naomi was very lonely. Soon, though, both of her sons married Moabite women, who gave up their own ways. For ten years the family lived together in Moab, and Orpah and Ruth, the wives of her sons, were loving daughters to Naomi.

But then the men died, too, and the three women were left alone. Naomi was sad, and she longed to go home after so many years away. Even in Moab, word had spread that the Lord had remembered His people in Israel, and she knew it was time to return to her place there. Orpah and Ruth started the long journey with her, but Naomi blessed them and said, "Go, return each of you to her mother's house; may the Lord deal kindly with you, as you have dealt kindly with the dead, and with me." Then she kissed them, and together they wept, mourning the life they had had with their husbands.

"Let us stay with you," begged Orpah and Ruth.

"Turn back, my daughters," Naomi told them. "I am an old woman. I have no husband, I have no sons. Go back, for there is no one here to help you through life and protect you."

They wept again. Then at last Orpah kissed her mother-in-law and said good-bye, and left on the long journey back to Moab. "Go with her," Naomi urged Ruth.

But Ruth said, "Do not entreat me to leave you...for wherever you go, I will go; and wherever you stay, I will stay; your people shall be my people, and your God my God."

Harvesting
The picture above shows women cutting and gathering grain during harvesttime. Poor people, like Ruth, would come later to collect any leftover grain. This is known as gleaning.

Naomi saw that Ruth would not be sent away. So together they went to Naomi's home in Bethlehem, where Naomi planned to ask a kinsman of her husband to take them into his family. The two women arrived at harvesttime, when the crops were being gathered.

"Go, my daughter," Naomi told Ruth. "Gather the grain that the harvesters leave behind in the fields." Ruth

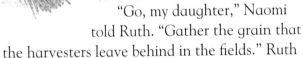

Ruth gathered the last of the barley.

went and worked hard all day, gleaning the little bits of grain that had fallen from the stalks. The owner of the land, Boaz, noticed her toiling in the fields and asked one of his reapers, "Who is that young woman?" The man had heard the story of Ruth's loyalty to her mother-in-law, and Naomi's loving kindness to her daughter-in-law, and he told Boaz their story. Touched, Boaz called Ruth to come before him.

"Stay here," he told her, "and glean all you can in my fields and eat and drink as you like, and my men will not bother you."

Ruth was amazed by his generosity; she fell before Boaz and asked, "Why are you being so kind to me?"

"I have heard of your loyalty to your mother-in-law," said Boaz. "Your reward comes not from me, but from the Lord, the God of

THEN SAID BOAZ UNTO RUTH, "HEAR YOU NOT, MY DAUGHTER? GO NOT TO GLEAN IN ANOTHER FIELD, NEITHER PASS FROM HENCE, BUT ABIDE HERE FAST BY MY MAIDENS."
RUTH 2:8

*While Boaz slept,
Ruth lay down on
the ground.*

Wheat and barley
Wheat and barley
were grown in biblical
times to provide food
for people and animals.
When the grains were
harvested, many kernels
fell to the ground and
were left behind for
gleaners to collect.

Israel." Ruth returned to the fields and gathered grain, more and more—because Boaz had directed his men to leave extra gleanings for her to find. When she brought the barley home to Naomi, there was so much that the older woman was overwhelmed and asked whose fields it had come from. "His name is Boaz," Ruth told her.

"Blessed be the Lord," said Naomi with joy. "Boaz is our near kinsman, Ruth. Let him protect you."

So every day, Ruth gathered grain in Boaz's fields, all through the barley harvest and the wheat harvest. When the harvesting was done, Naomi sent Ruth to Boaz in the quiet of the night. Boaz was startled out of his sleep, and cried, "Who is there? Who are you?"

She answered, "I am Ruth, your servant...and you are my near kinsman."

"It is true that I am a near kinsman," answered Boaz gently, "but there is one who is nearer still. If he is not willing to care for you, then I will." In the silence of the early morning, Boaz sent Ruth back to Naomi, and the two women waited for news together.

After Ruth left, Boaz went to find Naomi's nearest kinsman, the one man who could claim the plot of land that had been left to her by her husband. Gathering witnesses around them, he asked the man if he wished to claim Naomi's land. "I will redeem it," said the man, delighted at the chance to own more land.

"If you redeem the land," said Boaz, "you must also redeem and protect Ruth." For Ruth was part and parcel of Naomi's inheritance, and anyone who redeemed Naomi's land must also agree to care for Naomi and for Ruth.

"Then I cannot redeem the land," cried the man. "Take my right of redemption for yourself." And because it was the custom in Israel to confirm an agreement in this way, the man took off his shoe and handed it to Boaz.

Boaz held the shoe high. "You all are witnesses!" he said to the people gathered around.

So Boaz took Ruth to become his wife. Soon Ruth bore a baby, a boy she named Obed, and the women of the town said to Naomi, "Blessed be the Lord, who has given you this day a near kinsman."

Little Obed grew up to have a son of his own, Jesse, and Jesse grew up to have a son of his own—and that son's name was David. And David, the great-grandson of Ruth the convert, the great-great-grandson of Naomi, grew up to become the king of Israel—but that was many years in the future. For now, Naomi took the baby, and held him close, and she loved him very much, for he was her near kinsman.

AND WHEN BOAZ HAD EATEN AND DRUNK, AND HIS HEART WAS MERRY, HE WENT TO LIE DOWN AT THE END OF THE HEAP OF CORN; AND SHE CAME SOFTLY, AND UNCOVERED HIS FEET, AND LAID HER DOWN.
RUTH 3:7

SO THE NEAR KINSMAN SAID UNTO BOAZ, "BUY IT FOR YOURSELF." AND HE DREW OFF HIS SHOE.
RUTH 4:8

AND THE WOMEN HER NEIGHBORS GAVE IT A NAME, SAYING, "THERE IS A SON BORN TO NAOMI"; AND THEY CALLED HIS NAME OBED; HE IS THE FATHER OF JESSE, THE FATHER OF DAVID.
RUTH 4:17

Samuel Is Called by God

Hannah kneeled in the temple to pray for a child, as she had so many, many times before. But this time she promised God, "If You give me a son, I will give him to You."

The holy man at the temple, Eli, watched her. Hannah prayed from her heart, so that her lips moved but no sound came out. "May God give you what you ask," Eli said to her.

God did answer Hannah's prayers. When her son was born, she called him Samuel, which means "I asked God." In time, Hannah returned to the temple with little Samuel. "Do you remember when I was here last?" she asked Eli. "I prayed for this boy, and I promised him to God. Now I have brought him to you."

Breastpiece
Eli was a high priest and would have worn a linen breastpiece like the one above. It is inset with twelve gemstones, representing the twelve tribes of Israel. The breastpiece was tied to an ephod, a two-piece apron, which the high priest wore over his blue robe.

Eli watched as Hannah prayed to God for a son.

Hannah gave her son, Samuel, to serve God.

Teaching God's word
As a high priest, Eli would have taught God's word to Samuel. In the same way, our rabbis today teach us. The word "rabbi" means teacher.

Eli raised Samuel in the service of God. His own sons had no respect for God and treated His followers with contempt. But Samuel, kind and devout, was beloved by God and by all.

The years passed. Eli grew old, and his sons grew more and more unruly. One night as the household lay sleeping, Samuel heard someone calling to him. He got up and went to Eli. "I heard you call me," whispered Samuel.

"I was sleeping, Samuel," said Eli. "Leave me."

Samuel went back to bed, but again he heard someone calling his name. He returned to Eli; again Eli sent him away.

Then—"Samuel!" He heard it again! When he went back to Eli a third time, Eli knew that it was God calling to Samuel.

"If you hear the call again, answer. God will speak to you," said Eli, awed.

Samuel returned to bed, and again the voice called. This time Samuel answered, and God said, "Eli's sons have sinned, and he has not punished them. I will punish them in his place. No sacrifice will pardon them for their evil ways."

Samuel lay still till morning, afraid to tell Eli what God had said. But when at last he repeated God's words, the old man was silent.

Then he said, "God will do what is right."

AND THE LORD CAME, AND STOOD, AND CALLED AS AT OTHER TIMES, "SAMUEL, SAMUEL." THEN SAMUEL SAID, "SPEAK; FOR YOUR SERVANT HEARS."
I SAMUEL 3:10

While Eli slept, Samuel was awakened by a voice calling him.

The Ark Is Captured

The Israelites were at war with the Philistines once again. They won some battles. They lost some battles. The Israelites would capture a piece of land, only to lose it again a few days later.

After losing a battle badly, some soldiers of Israel started talking with the elders. "Why did God let us lose today?" asked one. "Bring the Ark of the Covenant here, and we will take it into battle next time. Then God will be with us."

AND WHEN THE ARK OF THE COVENANT OF THE LORD CAME INTO THE CAMP, ALL ISRAEL SHOUTED WITH A GREAT SHOUT, SO THAT THE EARTH RANG.
I SAMUEL 4:5

The Philistines found the statue of Dagon lying broken next to the Ark.

The Ark was brought, and when it arrived in the camp, the men shouted in celebration. Now God would help them to win every battle! The cry was so loud that the Philistines, far away in their own camp, heard it. "Why are the Hebrews shouting?" they wondered. When they learned about the Ark, they cried, "God will destroy us as He destroyed the Egyptians! Be strong, men, and fight! Fight, or the Israelites will make us their slaves!"

The Philistines fought so well that 30,000 men of Israel fell that day, Eli's own sons among them. And the Ark, the holy Ark of God, was captured by the Philistines.

A messenger ran through the fields to carry word of the terrible loss to the Israelites at home. When Eli, now an old, old man, heard that his sons had been killed and the Ark was captured, he died on the spot from his sadness.

Meanwhile, the Philistines took the Ark and brought it to one of

Dagon
The chief god of the Philistines was Dagon, god of grain and fertility. He is sometimes represented as part fish, part man, as shown here.

their own temples. They set the Ark down by the statue of their god Dagon. But in the morning, the statue lay broken on the ground before the Ark.

The hand of God struck the Philistines, who lived near Dagon's temple, and they began to suffer from strange sicknesses. The Philistines moved the Ark from place to place, but disease and suffering always followed. At last the Philistines realized that the Ark would have to be returned to the Israelites; it was leaving a path of death wherever they took it.

To honor God, the Philistines built a new cart for the Ark's return. Two milk cows pulled the cart, but no man drove it. The Philistines watched as the cows set off—straight for the land of the Israelites, all on their own. In Israel, workers in the fields stopped and watched in amazement as the driverless cart rolled on, bringing the Ark back home.

Ox and cart
The Israelites used trained oxen to pull simple wooden carts, like the one in the picture above. Valued for their strength, oxen were also used for plowing and threshing.

Looking up from their work in the fields, the Israelites saw the cart bearing the Ark of the Covenant.

King Saul

Saul and Samuel met on a hill.

Saul   Samuel

Samuel anointed the king with oil.

Horn and oil
Samuel anointed Saul king with oil contained in an animal's horn. It was a sign that Saul was chosen by God and belonged to the Lord in a special way. Samuel would have used olive oil, perfumed with spices and myrrh. The Israelites had many other uses for oil. They used it in cooking, to soothe cuts and bruises, for preparing a body for burial, and as fuel for lamps.

Israel's people had always been led by judges, because God was their king. But the Israelites were not content. "We want a king like all the other nations have," the people told Samuel.

God heard, and he told Samuel, "They have rejected Me as a king. Ever since I brought them out of Egypt, they have doubted me. Warn the people what it means to have a king, but they will still want one."

Samuel did warn the people, telling them that a king would take young men to be his soldiers and young women to be his cooks, that he would take the best of the harvests to feed himself, that in time the people would cry out against the very king they had demanded and God would not answer them. But the people still wanted a king of their own.

The very next day, Saul appeared in Samuel's village, far from home, hunting for his father's stray donkeys. "That is your king," God said to Samuel. The young man hurried up to Samuel and started to ask him a question.

"Your father's donkeys are safe," said Samuel. "Now come with me to the shrine, for all Israel has been waiting for you."

"For me?" Saul was surprised, but he went with Samuel. Silently Samuel anointed Saul with sacred oil. "God Himself has chosen you as king of Israel," he said. "Go home now, but stop at the hill of God. There you will hear wonderful music, music that will seem to speak to you alone. The spirit of God will enter you then, and He will be with you always."

Saul made his journey, and as Samuel had said, it was a different man who arrived at his father's home.

Soon all Israel was summoned to gather before Samuel, and he spoke to the people. "God has chosen a king from among you," he told

AND SAMUEL SAID TO ALL THE PEOPLE, "SEE YOU HIM WHOM THE LORD HAS CHOSEN, THAT THERE IS NONE LIKE HIM AMONG ALL THE PEOPLE?" AND ALL THE PEOPLE SHOUTED, AND SAID, "LONG LIVE THE KING."
I SAMUEL 10:24

Samuel called the Israelites together and told them that Saul was their new king.

them. He looked out across the huge crowd, and asked, "Where is Saul, of the tribe of Benjamin?"

God answered, "He is hiding among the baggage." The people brought him out, and he stood before them, tall and handsome, filled with the spirit of God.

"This is your king," said Samuel. "There is no other like him among all the people."

And the people cried, "Long live the king!"

But Saul was missing. Where was he? At last they found him, hiding among the baggage.

113

Saul's Downfall

The Israelite army defeated the Ammonites, freeing the city of Jabesh.

Saul summoned his entire army to fight the Ammonites.

Saul was a warrior king. Strong, powerful, decisive, he led his troops with great courage. But he made a great mistake. The Ammonites threatened the Israelites who lived at Jabesh. The Israelites wanted to surrender—but the bloodthirsty Ammonites taunted them. If the Israelites surrendered, Ammonite soldiers would gouge out the right eye of every Israelite. Desperate, unable to fight or surrender, the people of Jabesh sent out a cry for help. Saul gathered a mighty army and set out for Jabesh. His messenger rushed ahead, bringing a note for the Israelites: "When the Sun is hot, you will be saved."

Sure enough, by the time the Sun was high in the sky the next day, the battle was over. Saul's army had scattered the Ammonites and saved the people of Jabesh.

Saul had proved himself in battle many times. But the Israelites were still not sure that they had done the right thing

Samuel told Saul that he should not have lit the sacrificial fire himself.

AND SAMUEL SAID TO SAUL, "YOU HAVE DONE FOOLISHLY; YOU HAVE NOT KEPT THE COMMANDMENT OF THE LORD YOUR GOD, WHICH HE COMMANDED YOU; FOR NOW WOULD THE LORD HAVE ESTABLISHED YOUR KINGDOM UPON ISRAEL FOREVER."
I SAMUEL 13:13

in asking God to choose a king. Two years passed, and the Philistines were on the attack once more.

"Take the army to the border," Samuel told Saul. "Wait there seven days, and then I will come and make the burnt offering to God. With His help, we will triumph over the Philistines."

The army marched the next morning. Waiting for Samuel, the soldiers hid in caves and among bushes, behind rocks, in tunnels, anywhere they could find a space big enough to conceal themselves. Seven anxious days passed. Yet Samuel did not come. The soldiers were afraid, and some of them ran away. Now Saul worried. What if Samuel never came? He called for the offering, and he placed it on the stone altar himself, burning it to please God before he started the attack.

Samuel arrived moments later. "What have you done?" he cried, seeing the smoldering offering. "You should never have made the offering yourself! You are a king, not a holy man. Now God will seek another king, and all Israel will follow him."

Samuel turned away. Saul held the edge of his robe, begging Samuel to listen to his pleas, and it tore as Samuel walked off. "As this cloth has torn," Samuel said, "so has your kingship been torn away from you today."

Canaanite altar
The Israelites were not the only people to sacrifice animals on altars. It was a common practice in the ancient Middle East. The Canaanites made sacrifices to their gods on rectangular or oval shaped altars. These were made of uncut field stones, like the ones above. Canaanite altars were usually built on "high places," hilltop sites dedicated to the worship of the gods.

God Chooses David

It was time to find a new king for Israel. "Stop grieving over Saul," God told Samuel, "and journey now to Bethlehem, where you will find a man named Jesse. I have chosen one of Jesse's sons as king."

"If Saul finds out that I have gone to find a new king, he will hunt me down and kill me," said Samuel.

"Tell them that you are making a sacrifice to Me, and Jesse's sons will gather," said God.

"LOOK NOT ON HIS COUNTENANCE, OR ON THE HEIGHT OF HIS STATURE; BECAUSE I HAVE REJECTED HIM; FOR IT IS NOT AS MAN SEES: FOR MAN LOOKS ON THE OUTWARD APPEARANCE, BUT THE LORD LOOKS ON THE HEART."
I SAMUEL 16:7

Jesse's youngest son, David, watched over his flock.

Samuel blessed seven of Jesse's sons, but he knew that none of them had been chosen by God.

שְׁמוּאֵל א׳ טז

In Bethlehem, Samuel prepared the sacrifice as the young men gathered around. Samuel was sure that Elial, Jesse's oldest son, was the new king, for he was strong and tall. But no. He was not God's choice. What about Abinadab? He was not God's choice. How about Shammah? No, he was not God's choice. Seven of Jesse's sons appeared before Samuel. But God said, "None of these men will be king of My people. You see only the outside of the man, but I see the heart and the spirit within."

"Are these all of your sons?" Samuel asked Jesse.

"All but David, my youngest," said Jesse. "He is out in the fields, tending to my flocks."

"Send for him," said Samuel. "I must see him."

Samuel waited with Jesse's family. At last David came up, a healthy, happy-looking boy. He was still a child! Samuel was full of wonder.

"Anoint him," said God. "He is the one." And so David the shepherd, youngest of Jesse's many sons, was anointed, for he was destined to become the king of all Israel.

Shepherd boy
David was the youngest, and, therefore, the least important, of Jesse's sons. He looked after his father's sheep in the hills around Bethlehem. Out in all kinds of weather, his life would have been a lonely one as he led his sheep to good pasture, and protected them from harm. One story in the Bible tells how David risked his life by killing a bear and a lion that threatened the sheep.

Samuel anointed David as the next king of the Israelites.

David and Goliath

Saul's army gathered to do battle against the Philistines.

David used his sling to throw a stone.

Sling
As a shepherd, David would have carried a sling for protecting his sheep. A shepherd would place a stone in the sling's leather pad, hold the two ends of the sling, and whirl it around at high speed. When he let go of one end, the stone flew toward its target. Used by soldiers as well as shepherds, slings were deadly weapons.

The Philistines had declared war. Their troops were massed like a solid wall on the battlefield.

Their champion, Goliath, stepped forward. He was huge. In his bronze helmet and armor, he looked nine feet tall. "Why fight a battle?" he called to the Israelites. "Choose one of your men to fight me. If he bests me in combat, we will become your slaves. If I best him, you must become our slaves." Goliath stood and waited for an opponent. His body blocked out the sun like a tower.

Meanwhile, David was traveling from his father's home to bring supplies to his brothers fighting the war. When he reached them at last, he heard Goliath making his challenge again, as he had morning and evening for many days. "Who dares to defy the army of God?" asked David.

Overhearing, Saul called David over to him. David said, "My courage is strong. I will fight that Philistine!"

"You are only a boy," said Saul.

"I have killed animals that attacked my father's flocks," David told him. "God has saved me from lions and bears, and He will save me from this Philistine."

"Then go," said Saul, "and may the Lord be with you!" He gave David his own helmet and breastplate, but when David tried to walk in the heavy armor, with a sword dragging by his side, he could barely move.

So, without armor, David went toward the battlefield, pausing only to pick up his own stick and to place a few smooth stones and a sling

118

שְׁמוּאֵל א׳ יז

The stone struck Goliath in the middle of his forehead, killing him.

AND DAVID PUT HIS HAND
IN HIS BAG, AND TOOK
THERE A STONE,
AND SLUNG IT, AND
SMOTE THE PHILISTINE
IN HIS FOREHEAD.
I SAMUEL 17:49

Philistine army

Philistine head
The Philistines were one
of the Sea Peoples who
originally came from the
islands in the Aegean
Sea. They buried their
dead in clay coffins, or
sarcophagi. Strange-
looking human features
were engraved on the
head ends of the coffins.

in his shepherd's bag.

Goliath looked down, down, down on the boy. "Am I a dog, that you battle me with sticks?" he boomed.

"You battle me with sword and spear," said David, "but I battle you in the name of God. The Lord will deliver you into my hands!"

Angry now, Goliath came closer and closer. As he walked, the earth shook. But David was not afraid. He loaded his sling, then swung it, faster and faster and faster. The stone sailed through the air—and Goliath toppled forward with a mighty crash, dead. With Goliath's own sword, David cut off the giant's head and held it high, so that all could see that, with God's help, he had triumphed.

Saul Turns Against David

After David killed Goliath, his fame spread far and wide. Saul still did not know that God had chosen David as king, but he made David a leader of his troops and he sent him into battles, where he was always very successful. When David returned, the women greeted him, singing. "Saul has killed thousands, but David has bested tens of thousands!" they cried—and Saul was jealous.

One day Saul summoned David to play the lyre for him. Usually David's beautiful music soothed Saul, and David was happy that he could make Saul happier. But on this day as he listened, Saul became more and more angry at the chances he had lost, and he turned his anger to David. Suddenly—umf! Saul threw his spear at the boy. David dodged, and the spear clattered harmlessly to the ground.

David had escaped Saul this time, but Saul was determined that he would die. Saul thought, "I will send him into battle against the Philistines, and let them take care of him!" But again and again David led troops, and

Harp
David's harp may have looked like this one. Called a nebel, it is made out of an animal skin stretched over a rounded box. Or David may have played a kinnor, a small stringed instrument with a wooden frame.

David dodged Saul's spear.

again and again he lived, for God was with him.

Then Saul spotted another way to put David in danger. "Marry my daughter Michal," Saul urged him. "But first you must bring me proof that you have killed two hundred Philistines in battle."

David went into battle, and with God's help, he killed two hundred Philistines that day. Saul had to let David marry his daughter, but he was still angry and jealous. And soon after the wedding, as David once again sat playing the lyre, Saul threw his spear, trying to kill him. David dodged again, and the point of the spear went deep into the wall.

Yet another plan had failed! Enraged, Saul plotted to kill David that very night. Michal discovered his plans and told her husband, "Run, David! Run for your life!"

When he was gone, she put a statue in David's bed, covered it with his blanket, and put goat hair where David's head would have been. When Saul's men came, Michal told them her husband was sick and showed them the bed. It looked for all the world as if David were sleeping soundly, huddled up under the covers. Saul himself came, still raging, and tore back the blankets. When he saw that David was gone, he was more furious than ever. "I will kill him!" he vowed. "I will not rest until my enemy is dead!"

Michal helped her husband escape through a window.

SO MICHAL LET DAVID DOWN THROUGH THE WINDOW; AND HE WENT, AND FLED, AND ESCAPED.
I SAMUEL 19:12

Michal bundled goat hair under David's blanket to fool the soldiers.

David the Outlaw

David went into hiding.

Jonathan shot an arrow to show that David's life was in danger.

arrow

bow

quiver

Warning shots
The Israelites used bows made of wood and bone, and arrows tipped with metal, for fighting and hunting. A quiver held up to 30 arrows.

David hid in the countryside near Saul's home. Jonathan, Saul's son and David's friend, found him there. "Tomorrow night, your father will ask for me," said David. "Tell him that I went to my father's house. If Saul gets angry, warn me. He wants me dead, Jonathan."

Jonathan could not believe that Saul wanted to kill David—strong, brave, kind David. But sure enough, the next night Saul asked where David was. "I told him he could visit his father," said Jonathan.

Saul was enraged. "Fool! As long as David lives, you will never be king!" And Jonathan saw that everything David had said was true.

David held up a piece of Saul's cloak, to show him how close Saul had come to death.

In the morning, Jonathan went hunting. When he reached David's hiding place, he shot three arrows into the air, then sent his servant to find them. "The arrows are farther away!" he called to the boy, loudly enough for David to hear. "Run! Hurry! Don't stop!"

When the servant was gone, David came out of hiding. Jonathan told him, "One day you will be king, and my father knows it. He cannot destroy you." The friends wept as they parted, Jonathan to return to his angry father, David to become an outlaw, hunted by Saul wherever he went.

For many days Saul led his army in the search for David. David, with a band of followers, roamed the hills, always just out of Saul's reach. At last Saul's men, three thousand strong, camped close to David's camp...very close. When Saul went looking for a place to go to the bathroom, he found privacy inside the very cave where David's men huddled in the darkness. He did not see the men, but they saw him! He stood so close to David that David reached out and tore the corner off Saul's cloak—and Saul never knew that David was there.

As Saul left the cave and started down the hill, David called after him. "Saul!" he cried, and Saul looked up to see David standing at the mouth of the cave. David was waving a piece of cloth high in the air. What was it? Why was he—

Saul looked at the corner of his robe and suddenly knew how close he had come to death. "God delivered me into your hands, and you did not kill me," he said, looking up to David. Now I know that you are the true king of Israel."

Hideout
In a cave like the one above, David would have had the advantage of seeing Saul and his army approaching from a distance.

David and Abigail

Now David was safe from Saul. He and his band of men roamed the desert and the hills freely, helping travelers and protecting flocks from harm. When the time of the yearly shearing came, David sent men to visit Nabal, a wealthy man in Carmel. "Tell him that we have protected his sheep and shepherds for many months," he told them. "Ask him to send whatever he can to feed our band."

But Nabal was a cruel, harsh man. "Who is this David?" he said. "Why should I feed him?"

Hearing this from his men, David cried, "We will kill him for taking our help and not repaying us!"

He gathered men for an attack. But just then a beautiful woman appeared, with a train of mules heavily laden with supplies. Clever Abigail, the wife of Nabal, had heard

Fig cakes
Abigail brought David cakes made of figs. This sweet, seedy fruit formed part of the Israelite diet. The figs could be eaten fresh, or dried and pressed into cakes. Figs were one of Canaan's most important crops.

Abigail loaded her mules with food and supplies, then took them to David and his men.

She knelt before David, begging for his mercy.

her husband turn David's men away, and she knew that she must provide for them herself.

She fell to the ground before David. "My husband was wrong," she said. "Everyone knows that you are doing God's work. Please take this offering!"

"God has sent you to stop me from acting in haste," said David. "Go home now, in peace."

Soon after Abigail arrived home to find Nabal having a merry feast, overeating and overdrinking, almost in a stupor by the time morning came. Ten days later, he was dead.

David thanked God for stopping him from killing Nabal—for in the end Nabal had destroyed himself. Then he sent men to Abigail, to ask her to marry him. As soon as she heard their message, she rode out to meet David. And she became his wife there in the desert, in God's sight and with His blessing.

AND IT WAS SO, AS SHE RODE ON HER DONKEY, AND CAME DOWN BY THE MOUNTAIN, THAT, BEHOLD, DAVID AND HIS MEN CAME DOWN TOWARD HER; AND SHE MET THEM.
I SAMUEL 25:20

David's loyal followers watched and listened.

Wadi
Abigail met David in a mountain ravine near Carmel. A ravine, or wadi, is formed by a stream that floods during the rainy season, but remains dry for the rest of the year. When dry, wadis were used as roadways. Wadis are common in the desert regions of the Middle East.

The Death of Saul

The woman summoned the spirit of Samuel.

The spirit told Saul that he would be defeated by the Philistines.

Saul was frightened by the spirit's words.

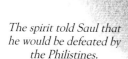

Sheol
The Israelites saw the world as a flat disk surrounded by seas and resting on pillars. Deep in the depths of the earth was Sheol, the resting place of the dead. Saul would have believed that Samuel's spirit was called up from Sheol.

The Philistines were on the attack once more. But this time, everything seemed so different to Saul. Samuel had died, a very old man, mourned by all Israel. Never again would Saul be able to turn to him for help. Now, looking down at the Philistines ready for battle, Saul felt fear for the first time.

Saul himself had forbidden the people from speaking with the dead. But he was beside himself with dread. He prayed to God but God did not answer him. So, disguising himself, he went to see a woman who was known for talking to spirits.

"I cannot raise a spirit for you," she said, not recognizing him. "You know that Saul has outlawed it."

"Saul will not punish you for this, I promise you," he replied.

She hesitated, staring into space. "What do you see?" he whispered.

"I see an old man, rising up from the earth," she answered. *Samuel!* Saul could hear him now.

"Why do you disturb me?" asked the spirit of Samuel. "God has turned away from you. Tomorrow, after the battle, you and your sons will be with me, and your men will be in the hands of the Philistines." Then he was gone.

Saul was truly afraid now. Yet he did what he knew he must do. He gathered his men, his own sons and his many troops, and he led them into battle against the Philistines. God was not with them on that terrible day, and soon the Israelites had fled. But still the Philistines fought. They were hunting for Saul and his sons. One by one Jonathan and his brothers were struck down, and Saul knew that he would be next.

"Take my sword," Saul said to his servant. "Kill me now. I do not want to die at the hands of the Philistines. Kill me!"

"No, no!" said his servant. "I cannot! You are the king!"

"King no more!" answered Saul. Seizing the sword he threw himself on it.

That night, Saul and his sons were with Samuel. One king's time had ended. Another king's time was about to begin.

Mount Gilboa
Mount Gilboa, shown above, was the setting for the horrific battle between the Israelites and the Philistines. The mountain, in what was northern Canaan, overlooks the valley of Jezreel.

Saul pleaded with his servant to kill him with his own sword.

127

The New King

The tribes of Israel bowed before David, the new king. "God has chosen you," the people said. David was thirty years old now, not a boy any longer, but a grown man—a man who had been filled with the spirit of God for many years.

David chose the bravest men of Israel, thirty thousand strong. He led them to the Ark of the Covenant, and they loaded it onto a new cart to take it home to Jerusalem. David and everyone else danced and sang as they traveled, playing pipes and timbrels, harps and drums, cymbals and sticks, anything that could be used to make music.

As the Ark entered the city, David spun and whirled and danced in front of it, and his wife Michal looked down from their home and

Jerusalem
Jerusalem, the City of David, became the political and religious center of Jewish life. The Dome of the Rock, a Muslim mosque, stands on the site of Solomon's Temple, the First Temple, planned by David and built by his son.

Dancing for joy
The picture above shows folk dancing in modern-day Syria. When the Israelites danced, it was a way of expressing their delight in God. On entering Jerusalem, the Israelites danced to thank God for their victory and to praise him.

The people danced as the Ark arrived in Jerusalem.

watched. The people settled the Ark in a special tent, and David made burnt offerings there. Then he blessed all the people in the name of God, and to each and every person, all those thousands, he gave a loaf of bread and two cakes. The people took their gifts home, and that was a day they long remembered.

But when David came home to Michal, she said, "You looked very silly dancing like that!"

"How could I have looked silly when I danced before God?" asked David. "To my last day, I will honor Him, and so I will keep dancing."

MICHAL THE DAUGHTER OF SAUL LOOKED OUT AT THE WINDOW AND SAW KING DAVID LEAPING AND DANCING BEFORE THE LORD; AND SHE DESPISED HIM IN HER HEART.
II SAMUEL 6:16

Michal watched her husband with scorn.

tabernacle

Ark of the Covenant

In his happiness, David jumped and whirled before the Ark.

David and Bathsheba

Bathsheba

David watched Bathsheba in her bath from the roof of his palace.

Bathing
This clay figure of a woman bathing dates from around 1000 BCE. After washing, Bathsheba would have rubbed scented oil into her skin.

David thought deeply about the Ark of God. "Is it right that I should live in a palace, and that the Ark should be housed in a tent?" he asked himself. "I will build a beautiful temple for it, here in Jerusalem, a tribute to God."

Still thinking about the temple and how to construct it, he walked around the palace, then up to the roof. He looked out and saw a lovely woman bathing. Sending messengers to bring her to him, he learned that she was Bathsheba, wife of the warrior Uriah. Bathsheba spent the afternoon with David, and then she returned to her home. Weeks went by, and then David received a message from Bathsheba: she would soon have a baby, David's child.

David sent for Uriah. They talked about battles and warfare, and then David sent Uriah home. But Uriah did not go home. Instead he slept right in the street near the palace gates.

"I told you to go home to your wife," said David the next day.

"How could I, knowing that my king and the Ark of God needed my protection?" asked Uriah. When the faithful soldier left, David

Bathsheba's husband, Uriah, was killed in battle.

Pet lamb
Generally, the Israelites did not keep animals as pets, but a lamb that had lost its mother would have needed special care. A shepherd, or shepherdess, may have taken an orphaned lamb into the family home to look after it, much as the poor man cared for his ewe lamb.

arranged with Nathan, the leader of his army, to put Uriah alone at the front of a battle. The very next day, Uriah gave his life to protect his king. And David brought Bathsheba to the palace to become his wife.

God was displeased with what David had done. Nathan said to David, "Once there were two men, one rich and one poor. The rich man had huge flocks of sheep; the poor man had only one little ewe that he loved like a pet. A traveler came by and asked for food, and the rich man would not share his own bounty. Instead he stole the poor man's sheep to serve his guest. What do you think of that story?"

"The rich man should be punished!" cried David. "The man who would do such a thing deserves to die!"

"*You* are that man, David," said Nathan. "Think. What did you do to Uriah? Did he deserve to be treated as you treated him? God is angry with you, and he will punish you."

David was silent. Then, "I deserve to be punished," he said quietly.

"The punishment will be terrible," said Nathan. "Your little son will die."

David fell to his knees, overcome. For many days he prayed and fasted, begging God to spare his child. But in the night, the baby's life slipped away. In time, though, God gave David and Bathsheba another son, a boy they named Solomon, who grew to become Israel's wisest king.

BUT THE POOR MAN HAD NOTHING, SAVE ONE LITTLE EWE LAMB, WHICH HE HAD BOUGHT AND REARED; AND IT GREW UP TOGETHER WITH HIM, AND WITH HIS CHILDREN.
II SAMUEL 12:3

The poor man and his little lamb.

131

Absalom

Absalom and his men rebelled against David, but were defeated in battle.

Absalom

He stayed near the city gate and talked with everyone who came to see the king.

Absalom liked to make himself popular.

Hair
In Canaan, men and women usually wore their hair long. This carving shows an Assyrian official with long, neatly curled hair. The Bible says that Absalom cut his hair with a razor once each year.

David had many wives, and they gave him many children. His son Absalom was a favorite with him. All day every day, Absalom would wait by the gates of Jerusalem, with his horse and his chariot nearby, welcoming travelers to the city. Everyone knew him, with his handsome features and his long dark hair, and everyone liked him—everyone, that is, except Joab, the general of the king's army.

Joab saw in Absalom all the evil that Absalom hid from his father. And soon enough, the day came that Absalom plotted against his own father so that he could take the throne.

From Hebron, a far-off city, Absalom sent word that the people of Israel wanted him for their ruler. Saddened, David gathered his men and fled Jerusalem. But after Absalom's troops had taken the city, David learned that his son had tricked him.

Both armies prepared for war. Before the battle, David spoke to Joab so that all could hear: "When you capture Absalom, treat him gently, for my sake."

As day broke, thousands of men fought for Jerusalem. With the struggle raging around him, Absalom rode out, watching the tide of battle. His mule passed under a mighty tree—and suddenly Absalom was dangling in the air, his thick hair hopelessly tangled on the lowest branch.

One of David's men ran to tell Joab. "Why didn't you kill him?" asked Joab. "I would have rewarded you richly!"

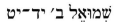

"Even for a thousand shekels, I would not have raised a hand against him," said the man, shocked. "King David asked us to spare his son!"

"I will take care of him myself!" said Joab. He rode out and soon found the helpless Absalom. Three spears to his heart, and the king's son was dead.

Then Joab blew his horn to end the battle, for David's men had won. David, looking out from where he watched at the top of the city gates, saw a lone messenger running toward the city. What news would he bring?"

Joab

Absalom's long hair became entangled in the low branches of a tree.

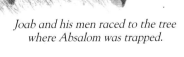

Joab and his men raced to the tree where Absalom was trapped.

Oak tree
The kermes oak, above, was one of several species of oak tree that grew in Canaan in ancient times. Oak trees are still found in the Middle East today.

"All is well!" cried the runner. "God has delivered the city safely back to you. Absalom is dead, and his men have fled."

David wept. "O Absalom, Absalom, my son," he said. "Would that I had died today instead of you."

"Stop that!" said Joab. "Your men fought bravely for you today. Do not let them see that your wicked son meant more to you than their lives."

The Wisdom of Solomon

AND THE KING SAID,
"FETCH ME A SWORD."
AND THEY BROUGHT
A SWORD BEFORE THE
KING. AND THE KING
SAID, "DIVIDE THE LIVING
CHILD IN TWO, AND GIVE
HALF TO THE ONE, AND
HALF TO THE OTHER."
I KINGS 3:24–25

*Solomon ordered that the
child should be cut in two.*

*One woman agreed
with the order.*

The other woman pleaded for her baby's life.

In his last days, King David summoned Solomon. "I am going the way of all earth," he told him. "Follow the laws of God and Moses, keep the commandments." Soon David slept with his fathers, and it was time for Solomon to rule.

Solomon swiftly took charge as king. And as David had asked, he followed God and kept the commandments. Then one night he dreamed that God came to him and said, "Ask, what shall I grant you?"

"God, you have made me king, but I am young to lead so many," said Solomon in his dream. "Grant me an understanding mind to judge Your people, to distinguish between good and bad."

God was pleased. "Because you did not ask for long life, you did not ask for riches, you did not ask for the life of your enemies—because you asked for the ability to give justice, I grant you a wise mind," said God. "And because you did not ask for them, I also grant you riches and long life, and glory that will last long after you."

Solomon awoke from this dream knowing that he would rule wisely. And he soon proved his wisdom, when two women came before him to judge their disagreement.

The first woman said, "This woman and I live in the same house, and I gave birth to a child. Just three days later, she also gave birth. But during the night, her baby died. She got up and took my son as I slept, and put her dead son in my arms. When I woke up, he was dead—but the child was not the son I had borne."

The second woman cried out, "No! The living baby is mine! The other was yours!"

The first woman insisted, "No! The dead boy is yours, mine is the live one!"

The king held up his hand for silence. "Bring me a sword," he said to his servants. When the sword arrived, Solomon said, "Now cut the live child in two, and give one half to one woman and the other half to the other."

The second woman said, "Give her my baby if you must, but do not kill him!" And she sobbed and sobbed, wringing her hands in despair while the other woman said calmly, "It shall be neither yours nor mine, cut it in two."

"The baby belongs to this woman who weeps before me," said Solomon. "Give the child to her. She is his mother."

King Solomon
Solomon was renowned for his wisdom, and this is shown in the story of the two women and the baby. He knew that the real mother would never agree to let her baby be killed. King Solomon wrote many wise sayings, and most of the Book of Proverbs is thought to have been written by him. Under Solomon's rule, the Israelites entered a golden age of peace and prosperity, crowned by the building of the First Temple in Jerusalem.

The baby was given to the real mother.

135

The Temple

Cedars of Lebanon
Large evergreen cedar trees covered the hills of Lebanon in Solomon's time. Cedarwood was valued for its beauty, fragrance, and strength.

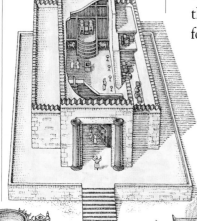

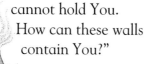

Solomon's Temple
Solomon's Temple, the First Temple, replaced the tabernacle, the sacred tent that was the home to the Ark of the Covenant. The Ark, flanked by two golden cherubim, was placed in the innermost room, the Holy of Holies. The memory of the First Temple is still cherished.

God had given Solomon great wisdom, wisdom beyond any other man. He understood all about trees, animals, the stars and planets—everything on this earth and off it, and he shared what he knew with everyone who wished to learn.

Because Solomon was so wise, his time was one of peace and harmony. He said to his advisers, "My father dreamed of building a temple for the Ark of the Covenant. Let us build that temple now."

Cedar and cypress and stone were gathered, and thousands of workers began to build the house of God.

Solomon designed the Temple himself, a mighty building reaching up to the sky. Bronze pomegranates along the top stood for God's bounty, and inside the Temple, rich gold was used for the altar, the candle stands, the fire pans. God was pleased. "I will live among the people of Israel forever," He told Solomon. "I will never forsake you."

At last the Temple was finished. The Ark was placed in its beautiful shrine. And a cloud entered the Temple, a gentle wind blew, and everyone gathered inside the house of God felt the warm breath of His presence. "Will You dwell on earth, O God?" asked Solomon. "The heavens themselves cannot hold You. How can these walls contain You?"

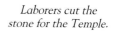

Laborers cut the stone for the Temple.

136

It took seven years to build the Temple.

Cherubim
The Temple was decorated with carved cherubim, usually depicted as winged creatures. The carvings may have looked like this Assyrian sphinx.

*The finest decorations were carved.
Nothing was too good for this holy place.*

The Queen of Sheba

Solomon's fame spread far and wide, so far that even the queen of Sheba heard of his wisdom. She had her servants pack up a long caravan of camels with spices, with gold, with jewels, and she came to test the great king's wisdom for herself.

Question after question she asked him. He answered every one. "There is nothing you do not know!" cried the queen, amazed. And she looked around her at the bounty that Solomon had gathered. Solomon's throne was made of beautiful ivory, decorated with gold,

The queen's journey
Sheba may have been in southwest Arabia. The queen would have traveled many, many weeks to visit Solomon, which tells us how widely his fame had spread. To get to Jerusalem, the queen would have taken the King's Highway, a major trade route controlled by Israel.

The queen of Sheba traveled to Jerusalem.

She was accompanied by a great caravan of camels, laden with spices, gold, and precious gems.

with elegant carved lions on each side. No other king had a throne like that, so fine and rich.

Gifts came to the king from all of the other great rulers of the earth, to thank him for his wisdom and knowledge. All of the drinking cups in the palace were made of gold. All the eating utensils were gold, too. Decorations were carved from the most exotic woods, brought from far-off lands. Embroidered robes in the finest silks and velvets, lovingly wrought weapons, chariots, horses, apes, peacocks—riches were piled high, beyond imagining.

"Everything I have heard about your kingdom is true, and more," the queen told Solomon. "All should praise your God, who honors your wisdom with riches and with peace in your land."

Precious gifts
Sheba became a wealthy land by trading spices, gold, and jewels. When the queen of Sheba visited King Solomon and brought expensive gifts with her, she may have wished to make a trade agreement with the king.

King Solomon came out from his palace to greet his visitor.

Mighty queen
Who was the queen of Sheba? Many cultures have myths about the powerful queen. Perhaps she looked like this regal woman from East Africa.

Elijah Shows God's Power

Baal
This bronze idol from about 1400–1300 BCE probably represents Baal, the main Canaanite god. The Israelites may have begun to worship Baal because he was supposed to control rainfall, which the Israelites depended on for survival.

Elijah appeared before Ahab, the king of Israel. "I bring a message from God," Elijah said. "You have brought this terrible drought on Israel. You have not followed His commandments. You have worshipped Baal and other gods who have no power to help you."

"You say your God is so powerful, but I have seen none of His strength," said Ahab coolly. "Show me His power."

"Call all the people of Israel here, then," said Elijah, and when all the Israelites had gathered before him, he cried, "Who is God? Is the Lord the true God, or is Baal?"

He and his servant prepared two piles of firewood, each one with the sacrifice of a bull above it, ready to be burned as an offering.

"Now call to your god, followers of Baal, and let him light the fire!" cried Elijah. The prophets of Baal called and prayed and begged and danced and hopped from morning till noon, but the fire did not

Elijah built an altar to God, and flames roared up from it

The priests built an altar to Baal, but it remained unlit

142

light. The wood was dry as tinder because it had not rained in many months, but still the fire did not light.

Then Elijah gathered the Israelites around his sacrifice, and told them to pour water over the dry wood. More and more they poured, until the wood and the offering were soaking wet and could never be lit by any man alive.

"BEHOLD, THERE ARISES A CLOUD OUT OF THE SEA, AS SMALL AS A MAN'S HAND."
I KINGS 18:44

Then Elijah raised his arms to the sky and called, "O God! God of Abraham, Isaac, and Israel! Show us Your power!"

A flash of lightning streaked to the offering, and a mighty fire roared up, blazing and crackling. In a moment, the wood, the offering, the ground, and even the stones around the wood pile were a pile of blackened ashes.

"The Lord is God!" cried the people. The followers of Baal ran for their lives.

"It is going to rain," said Elijah. He turned to his servant. "Boy, go up and look toward the sea."

"I see nothing," called the boy, looking from a hilltop. "There is just one tiny cloud, no bigger than a man's hand."

"That is God's power!" said Elijah. "The rains are coming!" And the sky grew dark and the water flooded down, soaking the thirsty earth. The drought was over, and God was back with His people.

Mount Carmel
Elijah showed God's power atop Mount Carmel. Carmel is the name of a mountain range that extends from the edge of the valley of Jezreel to the Mediterranean Sea. In biblical times, the mountains were covered in oak trees, olive groves, and vineyards.

The Still Small Voice

Jezebel threatened Elijah with death.

King Ahab told his wife Jezebel that Elijah had struck down the pagan priests of Baal with a sword—and Jezebel, who was a priestess of Baal, was angry. "I will have Elijah killed!" she cried in her fury. "Find him and slaughter him before me!" Elijah knew that he had done the right thing by slaying the false priests, but he was still frightened by Jezebel's threats. And so he ran away, far into the wilderness.

He thought about his troubles, how he was a hunted man, and he thought about how he had shown the people who worshiped a false god that the God of Israel was all-powerful. And he prayed that God would release him from his suffering. "It is enough, O Lord," he said.

Then, exhausted, he slept. An angel woke him and told him, "Arise and eat." There was food and water for him. Then he slept again, and again the angel came and told him to eat. After he had eaten, he found that he had the strength to travel forty days and forty nights to Horeb, the mountain of God.

In the darkness of a mountain cave, he despaired. How could he go on? Then God came to him and said, "Why are you here, Elijah?"

"The children of Israel have broken their covenant with You," said Elijah in a low voice. "They have destroyed Your altars and slain Your prophets, and I alone am left, and they seek my life, to take it away."

And God said, "Go, and stand upon the mountain before Me." Elijah stood on the mountain as God had told him. A mighty wind blew across the face of the mountain, and boulders and rocks fell all around Elijah. But God was not in the wind.

Then a powerful earthquake came, and shook the ground around Elijah. But God was not in the earthquake.

Then a great fire came, and the flames roared all around Elijah. But God was not in the fire.

THE LORD PASSED BY, AND A GREAT AND STRONG WIND RENT THE MOUNTAINS, AND BROKE IN PIECES THE ROCKS BEFORE THE LORD; BUT THE LORD WAS NOT IN THE WIND; AND AFTER THE WIND AN EARTHQUAKE; BUT THE LORD WAS NOT IN THE EARTHQUAKE; AND AFTER THE EARTHQUAKE A FIRE; BUT THE LORD WAS NOT IN THE FIRE; AND AFTER THE FIRE A STILL SMALL VOICE.
KINGS I 19:11–12

Elijah heard a still small voice.

Then came a still small voice. And Elijah listened to that voice, for God was in it. He wrapped his face in his mantle, and he went toward God.

Elijah's Final Journey

Elijah struck the surface of the Jordan River with his cloak, and the waters parted.

Elijah knew that death was near. "I am going on a journey," he told Elisha, his student. "And I must make it alone."

"I will not leave you," said Elisha, who loved Elijah like his own father. So together they set off.

When they arrived in Bethel, Elijah said, "Here I will leave you, Elisha. I must go on alone."

"I will not leave you," said Elisha. And they started off again. In Jericho, Elijah said, "Stay here now. God is calling me to the Jordan River."

"I will not leave you," said Elisha. So together they walked to the Jordan and stood watching the rippling waters.

Then Elijah took off his cloak and whipped it down, slapping the surface of the water. And as the Red Sea had parted for Moses, and this same Jordan had parted for the Ark, the waters parted to make a path for the two men, and they crossed.

"I must go on alone now," said Elijah. Before Elisha could speak, a chariot of fire, pulled by fiery horses, appeared in the sky and dove straight toward them. Elijah disappeared in a whirl of fire and wind, gone in a moment.

"Oh, Father, Father!" gasped Elisha, falling to his knees. "Do not leave me!" But he was alone.

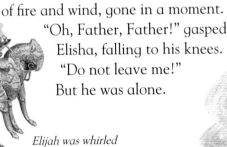

Elijah was whirled up into the skies in a chariot of fire.

Chariot of gold
This golden chariot and its four horses date from about 500 BCE. In ancient times, chariots were used in war and in important ceremonies. In battle, a chariot usually carried two men: a driver, who held the reigns, and a warrior, who carried a bow and arrow or a spear.

Elisha took up Elijah's cloak, lying on the ground.

Elisha and the Woman of Shunem

Elisha traveled all over the land, helping people and healing people. Often in his travels he passed through the town of Shunem. Watching him, a good woman there saw how he fed the hungry, how he had a kind word for everyone, how he truly followed God's laws. "Husband," she said one day, "let us make a little room with a bed, a table, and a chair for the holy man, so that he will have a place to rest whenever he journeys through Shunem."

The next time Elisha and his servant Gehazi traveled to the town, the couple welcomed them to their home. Elisha was touched. "You have taken so much trouble for us," he said to the woman. "How can we help you?"

The woman was quiet, but Gehazi knew what was in her heart. "She longs for a child," he murmured to Elisha.

"I understand," said Elisha. "In this season next year, your arms will hold a son."

"Do not mock me," said the woman. "My husband is too old for me to have a child now, after so many years."

AND SHE SAID UNTO HER HUSBAND, "BEHOLD NOW, I PERCEIVE THAT THIS IS A HOLY MAN OF GOD, THAT PASSES BY US CONTINUALLY. LET US MAKE, I PRAY YOU, A LITTLE CHAMBER ON THE ROOF; AND LET US SET FOR HIM THERE A BED, AND A TABLE, AND A STOOL, AND A CANDLESTICK; AND IT SHALL BE, WHEN HE COMES TO US, THAT HE SHALL TURN IN THERE."
II KINGS 4:9–10

AND HE SAID, "AT THIS SEASON, WHEN THE TIME COMES ROUND, YOU SHALL EMBRACE A SON." AND SHE SAID, "NAY, MY LORD, YOU MAN OF GOD, DO NOT LIE UNTO YOUR HANDMAID."
II KINGS 4:16

The woman listened as Elisha told her she would have a son.

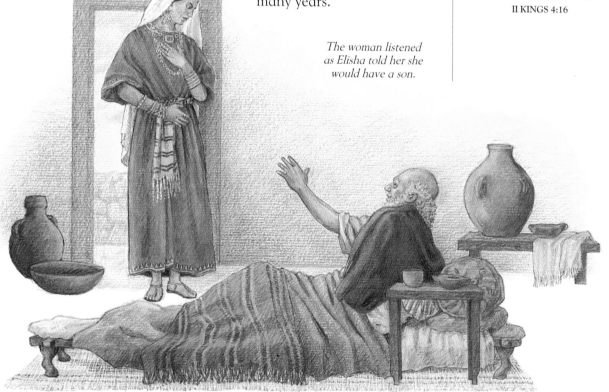

The servant carried the sick child back to the house and gave the boy to his mother. But by noon, her son was dead.

Shunem
The town of Shunem, now called Solem, lies in the fertile valley of Jezreel. It is just north of the town of Jezreel, near Mount Gilboa. Shunem was located on a well-traveled route, which explains why Elisha often visited the town.

"I speak the truth," Elisha said. And as he had promised, the woman had a baby the next year, a boy who was the joy of her heart and her husband's.

Elisha enjoyed seeing the baby grow to a toddler and then a young boy, for he stayed with the family each time he came to Shunem. Then one day, when Elisha and Gehazi had traveled to Mount Carmel, the boy was working in the fields with his father. The sun was high, the heat was beating down on them, and suddenly the boy fell to his knees, clutching his head. "My head, my head!" he cried in pain.

His father's servant snatched him up and ran to the house, where his mother took him and rocked him. His suffering was terrible...and then he died in her arms.

"Quickly," she said. "Saddle a mule. I am going to look for Elisha." She rode as fast as she could to Mount Carmel, where Elisha saw her coming from a great distance.

"What is wrong?" he called to her.

"My son—" she cried. Reaching Elisha, she slipped off her mule and fell at his feet sobbing. "Why has God given me a son only to take him away?" Elisha understood at once.

"Take my staff," he said to Gehazi. "Run to the house. Touch the boy's face with the staff. Run. Hurry!"

Gehazi ran as fast as he could, stopping to talk to no one. But when he arrived at the woman's house and touched the boy with Elisha's staff, nothing happened. After what seemed like an eternity, Elisha and the boy's mother rushed in behind Gehazi.

As soon as he saw the boy lying so still, Elisha began to pray to God, pleading for the child's life.

Then Elisha put his mouth against the boy's mouth, and his hands on his hands, and breathed life back into him. The boy's body seemed to grow warmer, but he did not move or stir. Elisha paced the room, praying again, and again he put his mouth against the boy's mouth and breathed gently. This time the boy's eyes flickered open, he sneezed seven times, and he sat up. His mother and father wept with happiness for God had given them their son once more.

After the boy's mother found Elisha, they hurried back to Shunem together.

Gehazi ran on ahead, carrying Elisha's staff.

Girded loins
Gehazi "girded his loins" when he ran to Shunem. This means that he would have put his robe between his legs and tucked it into his belt, like the Syrian workman shown in the picture. Laborers often did this to give them greater freedom of movement when they were working.

AND HE WENT UP, AND LAY UPON THE CHILD, AND PUT HIS MOUTH UPON HIS MOUTH, AND HIS EYES UPON HIS EYES, AND HIS HANDS UPON HIS HANDS; AND HE STRETCHED HIMSELF UPON HIM; AND THE FLESH OF THE CHILD WAXED WARM.
II KINGS 4:34

Elisha brought the boy back to life.

Conquering Nations

In ancient times, Israel and Judah were located in what we now call the Middle East. In biblical times, as now, this part of the world was often in conflict. The biblical land of Israel was right between two powerful kingdoms—Egypt to the south and west, and Mesopotamia to the north and east. So the Israelites were conquered again and again over hundreds of years, first by the Assyrians...then by the Babylonians...then by the Persians.

The Assyrian Empire ruled over Mesopotamia from around 850 BCE. Starting about 750 BCE, they became a constant threat to the northern kingdom of Israel and the southern kingdom of Judah. The northern kingdom was captured by the Assyrians in 722 BCE.

Proud of their pagan gods, including

Ishtar, the goddess of love and war, and many other deities, and proud of their prowess in war, the Assyrians kept careful, detailed records. In 1853, excavators in Nineveh found an ancient clay tablet that described a great flood that destroyed all life—a flood that is strikingly similar to the flood described in the Bible.

Over time, the Assyrians became less powerful, and in 612 BCE the Babylonians captured Nineveh and started to conquer the Assyrian Empire. The Babylonian king, Nebuchadnezzar, had control over Judah, and when the people there rebelled, he ordered the destruction of the city of Jerusalem and the

After the First Temple was destroyed, many Israelites were exiled in Babylon. But they never forgot Jerusalem.

A mighty army
Assyrian soldiers use bows and arrows, spears, and other weapons as they attack Lachish, a city that was eventually captured in the name of their king, Sennacherib. This carved panel, from Sennacherib's palace at Nineveh, shows the power of his army.

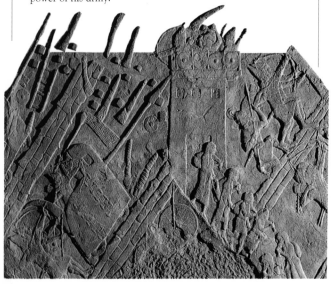

Temple there built by King Solomon. Around the same time, 586 BCE, Nebuchadnezzar forced many Judeans into exile in Babylon.

The northern entrance to the city was guarded from the elegant Ishtar Gate, covered with bright blue glazed bricks decorated with bulls and dragons. Two of the main buildings were a grand palace and a temple dedicated to Marduk, the patron god of the city. That temple stood at the top of a very tall ziggurat, a tower that looked as though it was built of gigantic steps. Some scholars believe that this ziggurat might have been the Tower of Babel described in the Book of Genesis.

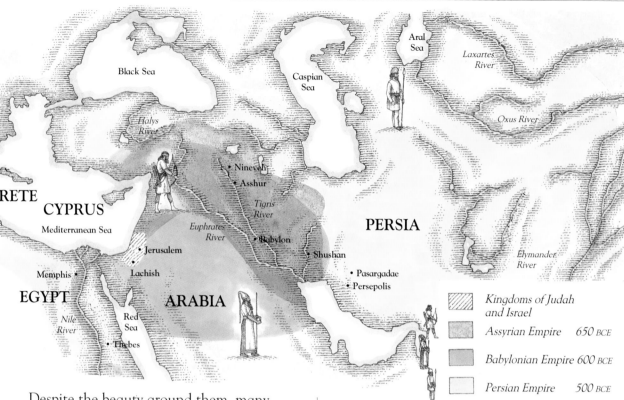

Black Sea

Caspian Sea

Aral Sea

Laxartes River

Halys River

Oxus River

Nineveh

Asshur

Tigris River

Euphrates River

Babylon

Shushan

PERSIA

Elymander River

CRETE

CYPRUS

Mediterranean Sea

Jerusalem

Memphis

Lachish

EGYPT

ARABIA

Nile River

Red Sea

Thebes

Pasargadae

Persepolis

Kingdoms of Judah and Israel

Assyrian Empire 650 BCE

Babylonian Empire 600 BCE

Persian Empire 500 BCE

Despite the beauty around them, many Israelites were unhappy. They longed to go home. They wrote about how much they missed Jerusalem, and while they were in exile, they began meeting to worship God in assembly houses eventually called synagogues—but the temple in Jerusalem was where they wanted to be.

The map above shows the three nations that conquered the people of Israel between 900 BCE and 300 BCE.

THE GATEWAY TO BABYLON

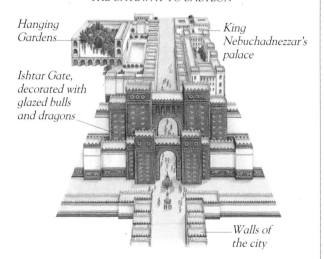

Hanging Gardens

King Nebuchadnezzar's palace

Ishtar Gate, decorated with glazed bulls and dragons

Walls of the city

A brick frieze of a Persian guard.

In 539 BCE, Persia invaded Babylonia. The Persian king, Cyrus the Great, attacked Babylon by diverting the Euphrates River and marching his soldiers up the dry riverbed. Cyrus controlled a mighty empire, and part of his success as a leader came because he sent exiles back to their homelands.

So, after fifty years in exile, many Israelites went home to Jerusalem at last. Today, Jews around the world still think of Jerusalem as the holy center of Judaism—at the end of the Seder meal and on special occasions, we say, "Next year in Jerusalem!"

Jonah and the Great Fish

"Go to Nineveh at once," God ordered Jonah. "Warn the people there that they must change their wicked ways." But Jonah did not go to Nineveh. Instead, he ran away. He ran until he came to the sea, and he got on a ship set to sail. But God sent a mighty storm after the ship, and the sailors were so frightened that each one prayed to his own gods—except for Jonah. The men said to him, "Who are you? What have you done, to bring this disaster down upon us?"

"I am a Hebrew," Jonah told them. "I worship the God of Heaven, who made both sea and land. But I am running away from His service."

The men were terrified. The ship was rocking and creaking, and the storm was growing stronger by the minute. "Save yourselves. Throw me overboard," said Jonah. "This storm came to you because of me." They did not want to throw him into the churning water; it meant certain death. But the storm raged on, and finally, desperate, they heaved Jonah over the side.

Suddenly the sea was calm. And a great fish swam by and opened its huge mouth, and it swallowed Jonah up.

In the belly of the fish for three days, Jonah prayed to

Whale of the deep
The "fish" that swallowed Jonah may have been a sperm whale. These whales are known to visit the eastern Mediterranean Sea. With their large throats, they can swallow the body of a man whole.

The sailors threw Jonah overboard.

Jonah was swallowed by a great fish, and he stayed there for three days and three nights.

God. "I called to the Lord, and He answered me," he said to the darkness all around him. "The waters closed in over me, yet You brought me up from the depths. What I have vowed, God, I will perform. I will serve You to the end of my days."

God commanded the fish to release Jonah on dry land. "Now go at once to Nineveh," God said. Jonah went, and in the town he cried, "Forty days more, and God will destroy Nineveh! Give up your evil ways!"

The people of Nineveh believed in God's power. From the poorest beggar to the king on his throne, they all immediately changed their ways. "God may yet relent!" their king told them.

God did relent. But Jonah was angry. "God, you are too good," he said. "Punish these sinners, or take my life, for I would rather die than live!"

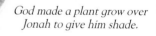

God made a plant grow over Jonah to give him shade.

"Are you so deeply grieved?" said God. Then he made a plant grow over Jonah, to give him shade as he sat on the ground. Jonah was very happy about the plant. But then God made a worm grow inside it, and the plant withered away. The sun beat down on Jonah, and he told God, "I would rather die than live."

"Are you so deeply grieved?" asked God. "You care about the plant, which you did not grow, which appeared overnight and perished overnight. Should I not care about Nineveh, a great city full of My children? Should I not spare them?"

Nineveh
The wall that surrounded Nineveh, the capital of Assyria, was enormous, strong, and sturdy, intended to withstand any army. This re-creation shows what it probably looked like.

Ezekiel and the Dry Bones

As Ezekiel watched, the dry bones came back to life.

"SO I PROPHESIED AS HE
COMMANDED ME, AND THE
BREATH CAME INTO THEM,
AND THEY LIVED, AND STOOD
UP UPON THEIR FEET."
EZEKIEL 37:10

God called Ezekiel to become His watchman, watching over the Israelites and warning them that Jerusalem would soon fall. "When you hear a word from Me," God told Ezekiel, "then give a warning." With Ezekiel's warnings, a person who had sinned would have a chance to change his ways.

Ezekiel went into the plain, as God told him to, and there the spirit of God entered him. He became a prophet, but he struggled to speak. When Jerusalem fell, Ezekiel used his prophesies to guide the people in God's ways, even when they despaired that Jerusalem would ever rise again.

Ezekiel had many visions; in one, God sent him into a valley filled with dry bones, the skeletons of the dead. God asked, "Son of man, can these bones live?"

"O God, only You know that," murmured Ezekiel.

"Pray over these bones, Ezekiel," said God. "Say, 'O you dry bones, hear the word of the Lord.' Tell them, 'Behold, God will make breath enter you, and you will live. He will put flesh and muscles on you, and cover you with skin, and put breath in you, and you will live. Then you will know that God is the Lord.'"

Ezekiel spoke as God had commanded him, and there was a commotion. The bones were coming together, bone to the next bone, and flesh and muscle grew on the bones just as God had said. They looked like men, but had no spark of life.

Then God said to Ezekiel, "Call the breath of life." So Ezekiel called, "Come, O breath, from the four winds, and breathe upon these dead." The breath went into the men, and they lived again.

God said, "Ezekiel, these men are like the Israelites. They say, 'Our bones are dried up, our hope is lost.' Tell them not to despair. Tell them that their God will lift them up. I will bring My people into the house of Israel once more."

Ezekiel bowed his head. "Wherever they have gone," said God, "I will take the children of Israel from among the nations. I will gather them all, and I will bring them into their own promised land."

מְלָכִים ב' יז–יט
II Kings 17–19

Hezekiah's Gold

Over the years, sometimes the Israelites followed God's commandments. Sometimes they did not. Sometimes they drifted very far from the laws of Moses. And so, the people were weak, because God was not protecting them. At last the country was overrun by the army of Assyria, and the soldiers took the Israelites to be their slaves—for the Israelites had forgotten what God had done for them when he took them out of Egypt.

For many years the people suffered. Then at last a new king, Hezekiah, came to power, and he destroyed the shrines to false gods. He trusted only in one God, the God of the Israelites, and he followed all of His commandments.

But Hezekiah's people were still slaves. He tried to buy their freedom, with all the riches of the palace, even stripping the gold and silver from the Temple. But the king of Assyria laughed at him. He told the Israelites, "Hezekiah tells you that God will save you, but He cannot save you! Did God save any of the other people who lost battles against my soldiers?"

"Be silent," Hezekiah told the Israelites quietly. But within himself, Hezekiah almost despaired.

"What should we do?" he asked the prophet Isaiah.

"Do not listen to what the Assyrian says," Isaiah told him. "God will help us. God is with us now. Pray to Him."

Hezekiah knelt down. "O God," he said, "hear us, see us, save us from our enemies."

"God hears you," said Isaiah. "And He says the king of Assyria will not enter Jerusalem. He will not shoot even one arrow on this city. He will return where he came from, for God will protect us."

That night, as the Assyrian soldiers slept, God struck them down so that they never awakened. When the king of Assyria looked out over his men, he could not understand why they lay so still, though the sun was climbing into the sky. He looked more closely, and then he knew. A broken man, he went home to his own country, and Jerusalem was safe once more.

Hezekiah's Tunnel
King Hezekiah once ordered that a tunnel be dug beneath Jerusalem, so that the city's water supply would not be cut off by the invading Assyrians. Today, water still flows through Hezekiah's Tunnel.

Silver and gold were stripped from the Temple.

Josiah and the Scrolls

Josiah was only eight years old when he became king of Judah.

Ashtoreth
This gold pendant (about 1500 BCE) represents Ashtoreth, or Astarte, the Canaanite goddess of love and fertility, and the partner of the god Baal. Josiah destroyed an altar dedicated to Ashtoreth.

The great Temple to God, built by Solomon so many years before, was old now. And with so many people worshipping idols and following false gods, the Temple had lost its gleaming gold and its beautiful carvings many years before. The mighty building, once the holiest place on earth, looked old and tired. But God's word is eternal.

And at last a new king, Josiah, came to rule over Jerusalem. He saw that by bringing the Temple to life once more, he could share the word of God with the people and bring them back to God. He set all kinds of craftsmen to work on the Temple, polishing and carving, building and fixing, all intent on making the sacred building wonderful again.

Then they made an exciting discovery! In a forgotten corner of the Temple they found a scroll, one of the scrolls where God's laws had been written many years before. Reading the scroll, King Josiah was awed and then saddened. How far the people had drifted from God's law!

Josiah brought the scroll outdoors, and in the place where so many generations of his fathers had stood, he began to read the words written there. Slowly the people gathered to listen, and the power

Many craftsmen worked to rebuild the Temple.

The scroll of the law was discovered.

Josiah read the scroll aloud, and more and more people gathered to listen.

All the altars to false gods were destroyed.

AND THE KING WENT UP TO THE HOUSE OF THE LORD, AND ALL THE MEN OF JUDAH AND ALL THE INHABITANTS OF JERUSALEM WITH HIM, AND THE PRIESTS, AND THE PROPHETS, AND ALL THE PEOPLE, BOTH SMALL AND GREAT; AND HE READ IN THEIR EARS ALL THE WORDS OF THE BOOK OF THE COVENANT.
II KINGS 23:2

Kidron Valley
The Israelites burned their altars and statues to false gods in the Kidron Valley, on the eastern slopes of Jerusalem. Later, idols were regularly destroyed and left here. The valley is also a place of burial.

of the words moved them. In the presence of the Lord, Josiah and all of the people promised to keep their covenant with God once again.

In the days and the weeks and the months that followed, Josiah destroyed the shrines to false gods and brought the people back to God Himself. And in the spring, for the first time in many, many years, the people observed Passover as God had told them, remembering how He had brought them out of Egypt to the Promised Land.

Jeremiah and the Potter's Clay

Almond tree
After God touched Jeremiah, He asked what he could see. "An almond tree in bloom," Jeremiah said. As Jeremiah watched the tree, God watches us. In Hebrew, the word for "watching" is similar to the one for "almond tree."

Jeremiah watched a potter sitting at his wheel.

God chose Jeremiah to be a prophet even before he was born. When Jeremiah was still a boy, God spoke to him. "On this day I set you on your journey, to uproot and to plant, to destroy and to build," God said, touching the youngster on the mouth.

God told Jeremiah to visit the house of a potter, a man who made pots and jars out of clay. Watching the potter working the soft clay on his wheel, Jeremiah noticed that if one of the pots got bent or damaged, the potter would stop the wheel and reshape the clay with his hands. Then it might be a pot again...or it might be a jar, or a pitcher, or a drinking cup, whatever the potter chose to make. Later the new pot or pitcher would be fired in the kiln so the clay would become hard and solid.

Jeremiah heard a voice. "Just as the potter shapes the clay, so do I shape the house of Israel," said God softly. "At any time I may start a new nation. At any time I may destroy what I have made. My people have forgotten Me, Jeremiah. Tell them they must return to My laws, or the punishment will be swift."

Jeremiah tried to warn the people that they should follow God's laws, but they became angry with him. "Save me, O God," prayed Jeremiah. "I pleaded with You to spare these people, but now I am afraid."

God told him what to do. When the people came for Jeremiah, he was ready for them. He had a jug made by the potter, already fired in the kiln so that the clay had turned hard and solid. As the mob surrounded Jeremiah, he lifted the pot high above his head, then smashed it to the ground. It broke into a thousand pieces. "Listen to me!" he cried. "God can smash you like this pot. He can break you like this pot. Give up your evil ways before He destroys you and your city!"

They left Jeremiah alone, but they did not give up their evil ways. And soon enough, God punished them. The Babylonians, led by their cruel king, Nebuchadnezzar, sent a huge army and

Jeremiah hurled a clay pot to the ground.

conquered the land, and many of the people were forced into slavery and marched to Babylonia in chains. The people who were left behind were ruled by a new king, soft and weak, and they all followed the rules that Nebuchadnezzar made.

"Look into your mind," said God to Jeremiah. "What do you see?"

Jeremiah closed his eyes. "I see..." he said. "I see two baskets of figs. One basket holds good figs, ripe and plump. One basket holds bad figs, too spoiled to eat."

"Those of My people who are enslaved in Babylonia are like the good figs. They will repent, and they will know My favor," said God. "The other people, those who have remained in Jerusalem, are like the bad figs. I will destroy them, for they will never repent. To them I will send disease and famine, ruining the land that I gave to their fathers."

Jeremiah bowed his head. He knew that God had spoken, and that God held the power of life and death in His hands.

God compared the wicked who repent to good, ripe figs. The wicked who do not repent are like bad, rotten figs.

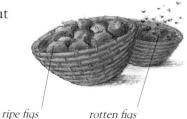

ripe figs   rotten figs

Potter
Pottery is an ancient craft. This Egyptian figure of a potter at his wheel dates from around 2500 BCE. Then, as now, potters "threw" their clay pots on a heavy wheel. They placed the clay on the wheel, then turned the wheel with their hands or feet as they molded the clay. God compared his control over people to the potter's control of clay.

The Temple Is Destroyed

"Leave Jerusalem!" cried the prophet Jeremiah. "The Babylonians are going to destroy the city! Everyone who stays here will die! Get out while you can!"

King Zedekiah's advisers were outraged at his warnings. "Stop telling the people to run away!" the advisers ordered Jeremiah. "You're going to scare everyone in the whole city!"

But Jeremiah would not stop, because he was spreading God's own warning to His people. God had told the prophet that the Babylonians would soon attack the city of Jerusalem. All of the Israelites who lived there were doomed.

But the king's evil advisers did not care that Jeremiah was doing God's work. "What can be done about this man?" they asked the king. "He is frightening everyone."

"Do whatever you think best," said King Zedekiah. "You know I cannot deny my advisers anything!"

Jeremiah was lowered into a pit.

The king relented, and Jeremiah was saved from the pit.

Zodiac signs
The Babylonians are thought to have invented the signs of the zodiac. The picture above shows part of a Babylonian boundary stone, built to honor the military services of a captain of chariots called Ritti-Marduk. The man firing the bow represents the ninth sign of the zodiac, Sagittarius, the archer.

So the advisers seized Jeremiah and threw him in a deep, dank pit, with no food to eat and no water to drink, and they left him there to die. Jeremiah's feet sank into the deep mud at the bottom of the pit, and he was trapped. This dark pit would be his grave.

But one of the king's servants, Ebed-Melech, saw what had

happened, and he saved Jeremiah. "No one should have to die such a terrible death," Ebed-Melech said to King Zedekiah. The king relented, and he sent his servants to pull Jeremiah out of the pit, grimy with sweat and mud.

Jeremiah had suffered in the pit, but he was not afraid. Even after his ordeal, he went on warning the people that Jerusalem would fall to the Babylonians—but they would not listen. And soon, very soon, King Nebuchadnezzar's army had taken the city. Just as Jeremiah had warned the people, there was terrible suffering everywhere.

But worst of all was that Nebuchadnezzar's army burned down the Temple that Solomon had built and dedicated to God in Jerusalem, so many generations before. Solomon's mighty Temple, David's dream, the first great temple to God, and the most beautiful, the most magnificent, the most holy, was gone, wiped from the face of the earth.

Ishtar Gate
This is a detail from the Ishtar Gate, built during King Nebuchadnezzar's reign of Babylon. Its glazed bricks were decorated with lions, dragons and bulls.

King Nebuchadnezzar's army took over the city, and they led Zedekiah away in chains.

The beautiful Temple in Jerusalem was destroyed.

The Israelites were taken to Babylon as slaves.

AND HE BURNT THE HOUSE OF THE LORD, AND THE KING'S HOUSE; AND ALL THE HOUSES OF JERUSALEM, EVEN EVERY GREAT MAN'S HOUSE, BURNED HE WITH FIRE.
II KINGS 25:9

The Fiery Furnace

Daniel told King Nebuchadnezzar the meaning of his dreams. In return, the king gave Daniel and his three friends important jobs.

Babylonian Empire
Under Nebuchadnezzar II (605–562 BCE), the Babylonian Empire expanded until it dominated the ancient Middle East. The Israelites were one of the peoples that were conquered by the Babylonians and moved far from their homeland.

"I had a terrible dream," said King Nebuchadnezzar to his wise men. "Tell me what it means."

"O mighty king!" they said. "Give us a hint."

He would not. "You tell me what the dream was about. If you cannot, I will put you to death. If you can, I will reward you richly."

"No man on earth can tell another's dreams," the men said. And so the king ordered them put to death.

"Wait!" said Daniel. "Give us one more night."

So Nebuchadnezzar granted them one more night, but what did it matter? No man on earth can tell another's dreams...unless he has God's help. Daniel prayed to God, and that night God told him what Nebuchadnezzar had dreamed—and what the dream meant.

The next morning, Daniel appeared before the king. "God knows all, and He has shown me your dream," said Daniel. "It was about the future. In your dream, you saw a huge statue, with a head made of gold, chest and arms made of silver, a body made of bronze, and legs made of iron. The feet were made partly of iron, and partly of clay."

"Go on," said the king. "What else did your God tell you?"

"As you watched, a stone struck the statue's feet. The whole statue crumbled to dust and blew away in the wind. And then the little stone grew to become a mountain," said Daniel. "Was this your dream?"

"Yes," said the king. "Now tell me...what does it mean?"

Daniel paused. "You, the king, have been given wealth and power in this life. You are the golden head of the statue. Another kingdom, not so strong, will come after you, then another, weaker still; those are the silver and the bronze times. Then there will be a strong kingdom, made of iron. The feet, iron and clay mixed, show that the country will be divided. At the time of this iron kingdom, God will use his power to destroy all earthly nations—that is what the stone means. And God's own kingdom will rise up in their place, a mighty mountain strong as the earth itself."

King Nebuchadnezzar was awed. "Truly your God is great, for He reveals mysteries," he said. And he made Daniel the leader of all of his wise men. Shadrach, Meshach, and Abed-nego, who served the same God, were also honored.

But soon Nebuchadnezzar had an idea. He built a huge statue of his own, made all of gold. Leaving Daniel behind in Jerusalem, he gathered all of his other wise men, all of his advisers, all of his noblemen, and he took them to see the statue, towering in the desert.

"Whenever you hear music," he told them, "you must bow down before this statue and worship it. Anyone who does not bow will be thrown into the fiery furnace!" Then musicians struck up a solemn song. Almost everyone bowed down right away— but Shadrach, Meshach, and Abed-nego stood proud and tall.

"Fools!" hissed one of the advisers from the ground. "Did you not hear the king?"

"We heard him," they answered. "But we do not worship idols. We worship God."

The king was enraged. "Kneel before the golden statue!" he cried. "Or I will throw you into the fire, and we will see if your God saves you then."

"God will save us," answered Shadrach calmly. "We will not bow down to an idol."

Nebuchadnezzar was furious now. He ordered the servants to feed the fiery furnace until the flames were hotter than they had ever been before. The flames licked the mouth of the furnace, and the heat was so intense that the air all around rose in curling waves.

The king ordered a statue made of solid gold, and then he commanded everyone to worship it.

THEN NEBUCHADNEZZAR CAME NEAR TO THE MOUTH OF THE BURNING FIERY FURNACE; HE SPOKE AND SAID, "SHADRACH, MESHACH, AND ABED-NEGO, YOU SERVANTS OF GOD MOST HIGH, COME FORTH, AND COME HERE." THEN SHADRACH, MESHACH, AND ABED-NEGO, CAME FORTH OUT OF THE MIDST OF THE FIRE.
DANIEL 3:26

"Now kill these men!" said the king.

Servants seized Shadrach, Meshach, and Abed-nego, bound them, and drove them toward the fire. Just as they pushed the men in, a flame reached out, and in an instant the servants burned to ashes. And Shadrach, Mesach, and Abed-nego were in the furnace. The king and his men could not look away. They stared into the heart of the fire.

"Did we not put three bound men into the furnace?" murmured the king. "And yet I see four men now, unbound and unharmed. An angel is guiding them!" He moved toward the furnace. "Shadrach! Meshach! Abed-nego! Come out! Your God is great!"

The three men came walking out of the fire. Not a hair of their heads had been burned. Not a thread of their clothing was singed. Not even a hint of smoke remained around them.

"How great is your God!" cried Nebuchadnezzar. "Surely His kingdom will last throughout the generations!"

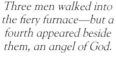

Three men walked into the fiery furnace—but a fourth appeared beside them, an angel of God.

King Nebuchadnezzar called to the men to come out of the furnace.

דָּנִיֵּאל ה ו

The Writing on the Wall

King Belshazzar was horrified by the sight of a hand, writing mysterious words on the wall.

Nebuchadnezzar's son Belshazzar became king after him. The new king planned a feast, and he served his guests with the beautiful gold and silver cups that his father had taken from the Temple at Jerusalem.

The wine flowed that evening, and guests drank merrily, toasting the gods of gold and silver, bronze and iron, wood and stone. Then suddenly the king, staring at the wall opposite him, grew pale. One by one the guests turned to look, and silence fell.

A human hand was writing on the wall, writing words that no one there could understand. "What does it mean?" whispered one guest after another. The king was ashen with fear. The wise men were summoned, and Daniel came at once.

"You used cups from the house of God, and with them you praised gods who cannot hear, who cannot speak. Yet the God who holds the power of life and death—Him you did not honor," said Daniel. "God sent the hand to give you a message."

"What is that message?" whispered the king.

"It says, 'You have been weighed in the balance, and found wanting,'" said David. "Soon, very soon, your days as king will come to an end."

Belshazzar was murdered that very night.

IN THE SAME HOUR CAME FORTH FINGERS OF A MAN'S HAND, AND WROTE OVER AGAINST THE CANDLESTICK UPON THE PLASTER OF THE WALL OF THE KING'S PALACE; AND THE KING SAW THE PALM OF THE HAND THAT WROTE.
DANIEL 5:5

Daniel in the Lions' Den

Medes
Darius was a Mede, one of a group of people closely related to the Persians. This gold plaque dates from around 400–300 BCE. It shows a Mede, possibly a priest, dressed in a tunic and pants and wearing a soft, pointed cap.

Darius, the new king, named many ministers and counselors to assist him—and one of them was Daniel, who soon rose above the others because of his spirit and talent. But the other counselors were envious of Daniel. "He's too perfect," they moaned.

The ministers and counselors proposed a new law, that the king alone should be worshiped, and if any man were found to worship another god, he would be thrown to the lions. And King Darius made it law.

When Daniel heard of the new law, he went to his house, where three times each day he knelt, facing in the direction of Jerusalem, and prayed to God. This day, he knelt down as always. The counselors burst in on him and dragged him before the king.

Darius was horrified, for he was fond of Daniel, and he tried every way he could think of to save him. But he had signed the law himself. And as the counselors and ministers reminded him over and over again, a law signed by the king could not be changed.

As evening fell, guards came to take Daniel. The king, almost in despair, said to him quietly, "Your God, whom you serve so well, will deliver you." Then Daniel was thrust into the lion's den, and a huge boulder was pushed into the entrance to block any escape. With a heavy heart, King Darius sealed the opening with his signet. Now no one on earth could help Daniel. The king retired to his room and spent the long night alone, fasting and unable to rest.

At the first light of dawn, King Darius rushed to the lion's den. "Daniel! Daniel!" he called, even before the den was opened. "Has your God protected you?" Silence—and then Daniel called out to him!

"My God sent His angel to shut the mouths of the lions," cried Daniel, "and so they did not injure me!" And when Daniel was released, no mark was found on him, for he had trusted in God.

King Darius made a proclamation before everyone. "All men must honor the God of Daniel, for He is the living God who endures forever, and His rule will last till the end of time itself. He performs wonders in heaven and on earth, for He delivered Daniel from the lions."

Daniel disobeyed the new law by continuing to pray to God.

דָּנִיֵּאל ו

Darius

Man-eating lion
This Phoenician ivory
shows a lioness gripping
a man by the neck. In
the ancient Middle East,
people were sometimes
executed by being thrown
to the lions.

*Darius was overjoyed to
find Daniel unharmed.*

Esther the Queen

Esther was so beautiful that Ahasuerus chose her to become his queen.

Many young women received beauty treatments so that they would look their best for the king.

mulberry juice

kohl

henna

Cosmetics

Esther may have used cosmetics such as the ones above. Mulberry juice was used to redden cheeks, kohl to outline the eyes, and henna to color the palms of the hands.

Perfume making

In ancient times, perfume was sometimes made by dropping flower petals and seeds into hot olive oil. The oil was then strained and cooled.

Ahasuerus, the king, was very angry with his wife. Queen Vashti had displeased him when she had refused to show her loveliness before the king's friends. Ahasuerus made a proclamation that all wives everywhere in his vast kingdom must obey their husbands absolutely.

And then he banished Vashti from him forever.

But King Ahasuerus was lonely. "Your Majesty," suggested one of his counselors, "gather all the most beautiful women of the land here at the palace, with their cosmetics, and then you may choose a bride from among them." The king agreed that this would be an excellent way to find a new wife.

Now outside the city lived a Jew by the name of Mordecai. He was the guardian of Esther, his uncle's daughter, an orphan. Esther was very lovely, with dark hair and dark eyes, and she was to appear before the king. "When you go to the palace, Esther," Mordecai warned her, "do not reveal that you are a Jew."

When the king saw Esther's great beauty, he loved her at once. So he set a crown upon her head and made her his queen. Mordecai watched over his niece from afar, and one day while he was visiting the palace, he overheard two guards making plans to kill the king. He reported them, and the king was saved. Mordecai's good deed was recorded in the annals of the kingdom.

Soon after, Ahasuerus selected Haman, an evil man, to be his most important counselor. All the other advisers bowed low to Haman, but Mordecai refused. Mordecai told the others that, as a Jew, he bowed to no man, only before God. Haman, enraged at Mordecai's defiance, plotted to destroy Mordecai and his people.

"The Jews defy your laws," he hissed to the king. "Your Majesty should not tolerate them. I will put ten thousand silver coins into the treasury if you will protect yourself and your kingdom by destroying the Jews."

Ahasuerus, tempted by the huge bribe and convinced by Haman's words, agreed. He signed Haman's decree, that all Jews everywhere in the kingdom should be exterminated—all Jews everywhere, men, women, and children, young and old, on a single day, the thirteenth of Adar.

Mordecai was horrified. Out of his mind with terror and suffering, he tore his garments and covered himself in sackcloth and ashes. Then, moaning and weeping in the streets, he went to the palace—where the guards refused to let him in, but took word to Esther that he was there. Mordecai's note told Esther about the king's decree. "Do not imagine that you, alone of all the Jews, will escape with your life by being in the king's palace," he wrote. "You must save your people, Esther!"

Ahasuerus
The Persian king who married Esther was called Ahasuerus in the Bible, but in history, he may have been Xerxes I. His reign lasted from 486 to 463 BCE. This Persian silver statue, probably of a king, dates from about this time.

Haman

Mordecai refused to bow down to Haman.

Haman became furiously angry and vowed revenge.

Esther Saves the Jews

Ahasuerus, unable to sleep, asked for the records to be read to him.

Prisoners' fate
This carving shows prisoners being impaled on stakes. Some translations of the Megillah, the book of Esther, say that Haman prepared a tall stake for Mordecai. Others say he built a tall gallows.

Appearing before the king without being summoned meant defying him, and defying him meant death—but Esther knew she would die with her people if she did not go to him. "I will plead with the king for the lives of the Jews," resolved Esther. "And if I perish, I perish. So be it."

When she appeared unannounced, she could barely speak. "Your Majesty," Esther whispered. "Tomorrow, come to the feast I have planned for you, and bring Haman as your guest." His heart melting, the king agreed. And when Haman left to go home, he was happy—until he saw Mordecai, sitting on the steps in his sackcloth and ashes.

"Tomorrow I am invited to a special feast given by Queen Esther," Haman told his wife. "But all my happiness sours when I see that Jew Mordecai. He will not bow down to me!"

"Build a tall gallows," suggested his wife. "And tomorrow when you see the king, ask that Mordecai be hanged on it. Then you will be able to enjoy the feast."

Meanwhile, Ahasuerus could not sleep. He tossed and turned, and finally he had a servant read him the royal records, thinking they would make him drowsy. Listening he remembered the plot against him. "Mordecai saved me, and I never rewarded him!" Ahasuerus said. Just then, Haman appeared.

"Tell me!" demanded the king. "What should be done for a man whom the king wishes to honor?"

Haman preened. "Who would the king want to honor more than me?" he thought.

"Let royal garb be brought for that man," he answered, "and a royal horse, and let him ride through the streets as the people cry, 'This is what is done for the man whom the king wishes to honor!'"

"Quick, then!" said the king. "Get the garb, get the horse, and get Mordecai the Jew, sitting at the palace gates." Stunned, Haman did as he was ordered, and soon Mordecai was regally parading.

אֶסְתֵּר ד~ט

That night, at the queen's feast, Esther had never looked
so lovely. The king said to her, "What is your wish? It shall be
granted. What is your request? Even to half the kingdom, it shall
be fulfilled."

In a low voice, Esther answered. "Let my life be granted as
my wish, and my people spared as my request. For we are to be
destroyed, my people and I."

The king demanded, "What man has dared to do this?"

"Our enemy is the evil Haman!" cried Esther, pointing. Haman
cringed in terror.

"Destroy him!" said the king. And soon, that very day, Haman
was hanged on the very gallows where he had plotted to put
Mordecai to death. The day that Haman had planned to destroy the
Jews became a day of triumph for them instead, a day for making
merry, for cursing evil Haman, and praising blessed Mordecai.

Megillah
We put on our costumes
and head to the temple
each year on Purim, to
hear the reading of the
Megillah, the Book of
Esther. Everyone loves to
scream and make noise to
drown out the name of the
wicked Haman. *Booooo!*
What was that name
again? Haman! *Boooooo!*

*Ahasuerus was shocked and angry
to hear what Haman had done.*

*Haman
recoiled in fear.*

*Esther told Ahasuerus that Haman
had plotted to destroy her people.*

Jerusalem Is Reborn

The king noticed that his cupbearer, Nehemiah, looked unhappy.

Silver cup
As cupbearer, Nehemiah may have served wine in a silver, horn-shaped cup, such as this one, tasting the wine first to check for poison. A cupbearer held a position of trust, and Nehemiah would have been an influential friend of the king.

Long years passed. At last, just as the Babylonians had conquered the Israelites, so the Babylonians were conquered by the Persians. Then a miraculous thing happened. The Persian king made a decree: "I have been charged by God to build Him a temple in Jerusalem," said King Cyrus. "All of God's people should help build the new house of the Lord."

Many Israelites set out for Jerusalem at once. But when they arrived, they saw that the beautiful city of David, once a marvel, was little more than a pile of rubble now. The walls surrounding the city had fallen. Thieves roamed the almost-deserted streets. And the great Temple, once the center of life for all who worship God, was just a few blackened walls. The new arrivals struggled in the hot sun with brick and mortar day after day, but the work went slowly, so slowly. Cyrus died, and Artaxerxes became king of Persia, and still Jerusalem was not rebuilt.

Nehemiah, a servant to the king, heard of the suffering in Jerusalem, and he prayed. "God, we have not kept Your commandments, but have You forgotten Your promises to my fathers?" he said. "God, hear my prayers. Let me bring Your people home to You."

That very evening, the king said to Nehemiah, "What is wrong? Why are you sad?"

"My people are working to rebuild of Jerusalem, but much help is needed," Nehemiah said. "My king, please—will you let me return to Jerusalem?" The king agreed, for God had heard Nehemiah's prayers. Nehemiah set off at once, bringing supplies and workers.

When Nehemiah had made camp, he saddled his donkey under cover of night and rode all around the city. Everywhere he saw desolation. He almost despaired. Surely Jerusalem was beyond even the reach of God. Then, as Nehemiah looked, words of God from the prophet Zechariah came to him: "Not by might, nor by power, but by My spirit." Remembering these words, Nehemiah knew that Jerusalem would rise again.

The next day, Nehemiah's men began work on the city walls, toiling every hour of the day and the night, with God's spirit.

And in just fifty-two days, the rebuilding was done, and the men stood looked at the shining new wall that they had created, with God's spirit. Broad and strong, it would protect the city and its people, with God's spirit. "Blessed are You, ruler of the universe, who has brought us to this moment in time," said Nehemiah, his voice rising to the skies.

Under cover of night, Nehemiah rode around the destroyed city, almost in despair.

Stonemason
Nehemiah would have employed skilled stonemasons to help rebuild Jerusalem. The mason hammered wooden pegs into holes in the rock, then poured water over the pegs. The wood then swelled, causing the stone to split. The mason sawed and trimmed the block with a chisel.

Ezra 1, 3, 5–7; Nehemiah 8

Ezra Shares God's Word

Thousands of Israelites gathered in Jerusalem to rebuild the Temple once more.

AND ALL THE PEOPLE
SHOUTED WITH A GREAT
SHOUT, WHEN THEY
PRAISED THE LORD, BECAUSE
THE FOUNDATION OF THE
HOUSE OF THE LORD
WAS LAID.
EZRA 3:11

From all over, people slowly came out of exile to return to Jerusalem, bringing with them all the gold and silver they had. The king of Persia himself returned all of the sacred pieces that had been taken from the old Temple long before.

Thousands of men and women, boys and girls traveled in long caravans. There were shepherds and farmers, gatekeepers and servants, teachers and hunters, priests and singers, everyone it takes to make a city.

As they arrived, each person stopped at the place where the Temple was being rebuilt, to celebrate that the Israelites were coming home at last. The first sacrifices were made on the new altar, right where the old altar had been, before the building of the rest of the Temple had begun. And day by day the crowd grew, and the work began.

Then cedar trees were brought from across the sea to be used in constructing the Temple. When the new foundation was laid, everyone danced and sang. Old people who remembered the First Temple that had fallen so many years before wept, and young people shouted aloud for happiness, and the sounds blended together and rose so that the

weeping and the shouting became one great sound of joy
and praise.

At last the new Temple was finished, a mighty structure ninety
feet wide and ninety feet tall. Ezra, a writer and priest known
by all as a great expert on the laws that God had given to
Moses, was summoned from far away to lead the people.
Ezra had set his heart on understanding God's words, and
on sharing them with others as well. "Blessed be the Lord,
the God of our fathers!" said Ezra. Then he gathered
leaders and good men around him, and with them he
traveled to Jerusalem.

The people of Israel gathered before the beautiful
new Temple. They were ready. Ezra brought the heavy
parchment scrolls that contained the teachings
of Moses and the laws of God, and he stood on a
platform built especially for leading prayers.

As Ezra opened the scrolls and unrolled them to reveal
the first portion he would read, everyone in the huge crowd stood
as one person and quietly waited to hear God's words. There was a
hush, long and deep, and all Ezra could hear was the soft drumbeat
sound of many hearts beating and the soft breath of life whispering
through all of the Israelites, joined together in one holy place on
this one holy day.

Then Ezra began to speak, and all who could
understand listened to him read the sacred
writings, from the first morning light to the
middle of the day, all of them murmuring
"Amen, amen" as Ezra read and read
and read.

Tears fell as they listened.
But then Ezra said to them,
"This day is holy; you must not
mourn or weep." And so the
people rejoiced on that happy
day, for God had given them
His own words once more.

THE OLD MEN THAT
HAD SEEN THE FIRST
HOUSE STANDING ON ITS
FOUNDATION WEPT WITH
A LOUD VOICE WHEN THIS
HOUSE WAS BEFORE THEIR
EYES; AND MANY SHOUTED
ALOUD FOR JOY
EZRA 3:12

*Ezra read the holy
writings to the people.*

Psalms and Poetry

King David is thought to have written many of the psalms.

Psalms

When David played the lyre, he would write poems that he could sing to soothe the troubled Saul and to honor God. These songs are called psalms, and many of the psalms featured in the Bible are said to have been written by David himself.

When I behold Your heavens, the work of Your fingers,
the Moon and the stars, which You have established;
What is man, that You are mindful of him?
And the son of man, that You think of him?
Yet You have made him but little lower than the angels,
and have crowned him with glory and honor.
You have made him to rule over the works of Your hands.
You have put all things under his feet:
Sheep and oxen, all of them,
Yes, and the beasts of the field,
The fowl of the air, and the fish of the sea,
all that passes through the paths of the seas.
O Lord, our Lord, how glorious is Your name in all
the earth!
from Psalm 8

The Lord is my rock, and my fortress, and my deliverer;
my God, my rock, in Him I take refuge;
my shield, and my horn of salvation, my high tower.
Praised, I cry, is the Lord,
and I am saved from my enemies.
from Psalm 18, the Song of David

The Lord is my shepherd, I shall not want.
He makes me to lie down in green pastures;
He leads me beside the still waters
He restores my soul;
He guides me in straight paths for His name's sake.
Yea, though I walk through the valley of the shadow of death,
I will fear no evil,
for You are with me;
Your rod and Your staff, they comfort me.
You prepare a table before me in the presence of my enemies;
You have anointed my head with oil, my cup runs over.
Surely goodness and mercy shall follow me all the days of my life;
and I shall dwell in the house of the Lord forever.
Psalm 23

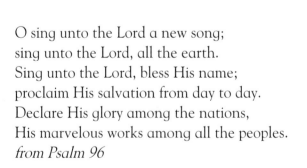

O sing unto the Lord a new song;
sing unto the Lord, all the earth.
Sing unto the Lord, bless His name;
proclaim His salvation from day to day.
Declare His glory among the nations,
His marvelous works among all the peoples.
from Psalm 96

Happy are they that are upright in the way,
who walk in the law of the Lord.
Happy are they that keep His testimonies,
that seek Him with the whole heart.
from Psalm 119

Psalm 23 compares God to a shepherd, guiding His people.

Ecclesiastes

It is said that Ecclesiastes was written by Solomon, the son of David and one of the wisest kings in history.

To every thing there is a season,
and a time to every purpose under the heaven:
A time to be born, and a time to die;
a time to plant, and a time to pluck up that which is planted;
A time to kill, and a time to heal;
a time to break down, and a time to build up;
A time to weep, and a time to laugh;
a time to mourn, and a time to dance;
A time to cast away stones, and a time to gather stones together;
a time to embrace, and a time to refrain from embracing;
A time to seek, and a time to lose;
a time to keep, and a time to cast away;
A time to rend, and a time to sew;
a time to keep silence, and a time to speak;
A time to love, and a time to hate;
a time for war, and a time for peace.
from Ecclesiastes 3

Proverbs

Proverbs, another book of the Bible that is said to have been written by King Solomon, gives us ideas for honoring God in our everyday lives.

Happy is the man that finds wisdom,
and the man that obtains understanding.
For the coin of it is better than the coin of silver,
and the gain of it greater than fine gold.
She is more precious than rubies;
and all the things you can desire are not to be compared unto her.
Length of days is in her right hand;
in her left hand are riches and honor.
Her ways are ways of pleasantness,
and all her paths are peace.
She is a tree of life to them that lay hold upon her,
and happy is every one that holds her fast.
from Proverbs 3

Songs of Songs

Solomon was not only wise; he was loving, too. It is said that he wrote The Song of Songs, a book of the Bible that includes some of the greatest love poetry ever written.

My beloved spoke, and said unto me,
"Rise up, my love, my fair one, and come away.
For, lo, the winter is past.
The rain is over and gone;
The flowers appear on the earth;
the time of singing is come,
and the voice of the turtle is heard in our land;
The fig tree puts forth her green figs,
and the vines in blossom give forth their fragrance.
Arise, my fair one, my love, and come away."
from Song of Songs 2

Who's Who in the Bible Stories

Moses and Aaron asked Pharaoh to let their people go, but he refused.

Aaron Moses' older brother. He spoke clearly and persuasively, and Moses did not. So he spoke for Moses before Pharaoh.

Abed-nego One of the three friends of Daniel, Abed-nego (originally called Azariah) was sent into the fiery furnace by Nebuchadnezzar.

Abinadab One of David's brothers.

Abel Adam and Eve's second son, and the brother of Cain.

Abigail One of King David's wives.

Abraham/Abram Abraham, the great patriarch of Judaism, entered into a covenant with God that has lasted through the generations. He was called Abram until God told him to change his name.

Absalom King David's beloved son.

Adam The first man, created by God.

Ahab A king of Israel at the time of Elijah. He was married to Jezebel.

Ahasuerus King Ahasuerus of Persia made Esther his queen. No one is sure which king of Persia he really was. He might have been Xerxes I, or he might have been a king named Artaxerxes II.

Asher The eighth of Jacob's sons. His mother was Zilpah.

Baal Baal means "master" and is sometimes used to mean the pagan god of rain, thunder, and fertility. Most of the time the Bible uses it as a general name for any pagan god.

Balaam A seer who was hired to curse the Israelites, but instead blesses them.

Balak The evil king of Moab who hired Balaam to curse the Israelites.

Bathsheba A wife of King David, renowned for her beauty, and the mother of Solomon.

Belshazzar A son of Nebuchadnezzar, and the last king of Babylon.

Benjamin The youngest of Jacob's twelve sons. Like Joseph, his mother was Rachel.

Boaz The near kinsman of Naomi. Boaz married Ruth and became the great-grandfather of David.

Cain The first son of Adam and Eve.

Caleb One of the spies sent to scout the Promised Land, rewarded for his trust in God.

Cyrus The king of Babylon who sent the Jews home to Jerusalem.

Dan The fifth of Jacob's sons. His mother was Bilhah.

Daniel An Israelite adviser to the king of Babylon, with a gift for interpreting dreams.

Darius A king of the Medes who ruled Babylon.

David A shepherd boy from Bethlehem, chosen by God to become the king of Israel.

Delilah Samson's wife, a Philistine who betrayed him.

Eli The high priest who raised Samuel to serve God.

Elial One of David's brothers.

Elijah The prophet who revealed God's power in a contest with Baal.

Elisha Elijah's follower and a prophet.

King Ahasuerus chose Esther to be his queen.

Esau Jacob's hairy twin brother, son of Rebekah and Isaac.

Esther The young queen who saved the Jewish people from the plotting of the evil Haman.

David killed Goliath with a stone.

Ezekiel The prophet Ezekiel prophesied over the bones of the dead and, with God's help, they rose to live again.

Ezra The priest and scribe Ezra read the laws of God to the people when the Temple was rebuilt.

Eve The first woman.

Gad The seventh of Jacob's sons. His mother was Zilpah.

Gehazi Elisha's faithful servant.

Gideon A leader whose tiny army defeated the Midianites, with God's help.

Goliath The fearsome giant who was killed by David.

Hagar Sarah's servant, and the mother of Ishmael.

Haman In the Purim story, the villain who planned to exterminate the Jews. Booooooo!

Hannah Samuel's mother.

Hezekiah A king of Judah.

Isaac Son of Abraham and Sarah, husband of Rebekah, father of Jacob and Esau, one of the great patriarchs of Judaism.

Isaiah The prophet Isaiah advised King Hezekiah.

Ishmael The son of Hagar and Abraham.

Israel After wrestling with the angel, Jacob earned this new name for himself and his people, the Israelites.

Issachar The ninth of Jacob's sons. His mother was Leah.

Jacob One of Isaac's twin sons, the father of the twelve tribes of Israel and a patriarch of Judaism.

Jeremiah A prophet of God whose warnings were usually ignored by the people. "You will go to them," God told him. "But they will not listen to you."

Jeroboam Solomon's son Jeroboam became king of Israel.

Jesse The father of David.

Jezebel A queen of ancient Israel. She killed God's prophets—but Elijah escaped her threats.

Joab The commander of King David's army.

Jonah Trying to run away from God, Jonah was swallowed by a great fish.

Jonathan Son of King Saul, Jonathan was David's good friend.

Joseph Jacob's favorite son. His brothers sold him into slavery, but his gift for interpreting dreams

helped him rise to power in Egypt.

Joshua After Moses died, Joshua led the Israelites to the Promised Land.

Josiah A king of Judah, part of Israel named after one of Jacob's sons.

Judah One of Jacob's twelve sons.

Laban Rebekah's brother, and the father of Rachel and Leah.

Leah One of Jacob's wives, the mother of six of his sons, and a matriarch of Judaism. The Bible says she had "tender eyes."

Levi The third of Jacob's sons. His mother was Leah.

Lot Abraham's nephew, head of the only family to survive the destruction of Sodom and Gomorrah.

Meshach One of Daniel's friends, who survives the fiery furnace.

Michal The wife of King David and the daughter of Saul.

Miriam The sister of Moses and Aaron, who celebrated crossing the Red Sea with singing and timbrels.

Mordecai Esther's cousin and her adviser.

Moses The great leader of our people. He led the slaves out of Egypt to the Promised Land, guided by God. When he came down from Mount Sinai, the people saw that "the skin of his face shone" from the joy of talking to God.

Nabal Abigail's husband.

Naomi The mother-in-law of the devoted Ruth.

Naphtali The sixth of Jacob's sons. His mother was Bilhah.

Nathan The prophet who delivered God's word to David.

Samson tore the lion apart with his bare hands.

Nebuchadnezzar The Babylonian king who captured Jerusalem and sent the people of Judah into exile.

Nehemiah The rebuilder of Jerusalem. He brought the people back from exile in Babylon to restore the temple and the city.

Noah Told by God to build an ark, he saved the animals from the flood. The Bible tells us that "Noah found grace in the eyes of the Lord...and Noah walked with God."

Obed Obed, the son of Ruth and Boaz, was David's grandfather.

Orpah Naomi's daughter-in-law, who returns to her own homeland.

Pharaoh In biblical times, the leader of Egypt was called the pharaoh. The pharaoh who made Joseph a powerful leader lived hundreds of years before the pharaoh who would not let Moses' people go.

Potiphar The Egyptian noble served by Joseph. Potiphar's wife made sure that Joseph was put in jail—but soon he rose to serve the Pharaoh.

The Queen of Sheba The elegant queen who was dazzled by Solomon's wisdom and wealth.

Rachel Jacob's beloved wife, mother of Joseph and Benjamin, and a matriarch of the Jewish people.

Rahab The Canaanite woman who helped Joshua's spies, and was rewarded by being spared in the battle for Jericho.

Rebekah The wife of Isaac and mother of Jacob and Esau. A matriarch of Judaism.

Rehoboam Solomon's son Rehoboam became king of Judah.

Reuben The oldest of Jacob's twelve sons.

Ruth The devoted daughter-in-law of Naomi, and David's great-grandmother.

Samson An Israelite hero who performed mighty feats of strength.

Samuel The prophet who anointed Saul and David, the first two kings of Israel. His mother was Hannah, who said about him, "For this child I have prayed... therefore also I have lent him to the Lord."

Sarah/Sarai Abraham's wife, and the mother of Isaac. A matriarch of the Jewish people.

Saul The first king of Israel.

Shadrach One of Daniel's three friends who survived the fiery furnace with his faith in God.

Shammah One of David's brothers.

Simeon Simeon was the second of Jacob's sons. His mother was Leah.

Solomon The son of King David, and the wisest king ever to rule over Israel. He built the temple in Jerusalem.

Uriah Bathsheba's husband, the faithful soldier who was sent to his death by King David.

Vashti The queen who would not show her beauty when Ahasuerus commanded her.

Zebulun The tenth of Jacob's sons. His mother was Leah.

Zedekiah The last king of Judah.

Zipporah Zipporah was married to Moses.

When the Babylonians took over Jerusalem, they led King Zedekiah away in chains.

Places in the Bible Stories

Arabia Ishmaelite traders (descended from Ishmael, the son of Abraham and Hagar) carried goods from Arabia to Egypt. On one trip, Joseph's brothers sold him into slavery for twenty pieces of silver. Later, the Ishmaelites sold Joseph to Potiphar.

Arabian Desert A desert to the east of Moab.

Asher One of the twelve kingdoms of Israel, named after Asher, the son of Jacob and Zilpah.

Assur The capital of Assyria. There was a large temple in this town, where the Assyrians worshipped their gods, including the god Assur.

Assyria An ancient country near the Tigris River. Assyria was at war with Israel for many years.

Babel Traditionally, Babel, the site of the Tower of Babel, is thought to be Babylon.

Babylon The mighty city of Babylon was renowned for its Hanging Gardens. After Jerusalem was destroyed, the Israelites were taken as captives to Babylon, where they lived as exiles for many years. In Babylon, Daniel's three friends faced the fiery furnace, King Belshazzar saw the writing on the wall, and Daniel was thrown to the lions.

Babylonia The ancient country located between the southern Tigris and Euphrates Rivers. Babylon was the capital.

Beersheba (desert) Beersheba is thought to mean "well of the oath," and the area may have been the place where Abraham and the Philistine king Abimelech pledged to keep the peace between their peoples. This desert is the place where Ishmael almost died, and God's angel showed Hagar the spring that saved him.

Beersheba (town) Abraham settled in the town of Beersheba at the end of his journey to Canaan. Isaac and Rebekah lived there, with Jacob and Esau, until Jacob tricked Esau and ran away. Today Beersheba (usually spelled Be'er-Sheva now) is one of the largest cities in Israel.

Ben Hinnom In this valley, Jeremiah smashed a clay jar and predicted that God would destroy the wicked Judeans.

Benjamin One of the original twelve kingdoms of Israel, named after the youngest son of Rachel and Jacob.

Bethel On a journey from Beersheba to Haran, Jacob dreamed of a ladder to God, a staircase reaching right up to the heavens. He named the spot where he had the dream Bethel, after the word for a meeting place. Today many synagogues are named for this holy place.

Bethlehem After she was widowed, Naomi traveled back to her home in Bethlehem, with her devoted daughter-in-law Ruth. David was later born here.

Brook of Kerith God told Elijah to hide near the brook so that he would have water even in a drought.

Canaan Canaan means "the promised land." Abraham and his people settled here, after leaving Ur and then Haran. His grandson Jacob lived here, too, with his twelve sons, but during the great famine, most of the family went to Egypt. After forty years of wandering in the wilderness, the Israelites settled here. Later, the kingdom was divided into two parts: Israel in the north, and Judah in the south.

Damascus Damascus, the capital of Syria, may be the oldest continuously populated city in the world. Archeological clues tell us that there were people living here as long ago as 10,000 BCE. Jacob passed through the city on his way to Haran.

Dan One of the twelve original kingdoms of Israel, named after Dan, the son of Jacob and Bilhah.

The Jezreel Valley (shown here) is in the northern part of Canaan.

Dead Sea The Jordan River flows into the Dead Sea, the deepest hypersaline ("overly salty") sea in the world. King David journeyed there to relax.

The Dead Sea contains so much salt that nothing can live there.

Edom Edom is the same word as Esau, and the country where Esau's people settled is called Edom. It was south of Moab.

Egypt Joseph was taken to Egypt by the Ishmaelites after his brothers sold him into slavery. There he interpreted the pharaoh's dreams and rose to become a high official, rescuing the people from famine. In time he brought most of his brothers to Egypt from Canaan. Hundreds of years later, in Moses' time, the Israelites were the slaves of the Pharaoh. God was forced to bring the ten plagues down on the Egyptians before Pharaoh would allow the Israelites to leave.

Endor The witch at Endor summoned up the spirit of Samuel. The ghost told Saul he would be defeated by the Philistines.

En-Gedi When David was an outlaw, running from Saul, he and his men hid in a cave at the oasis of En-Gedi. The Bible is very specific: "And David went up from thence, and dwelt in the strongholds of En-Gedi." (I Samuel 24:1)

Ephraim One of the original twelve kingdoms of Israel, named after the second son of Joseph. Jacob blessed Ephraim and Manasseh, his older brother, when Joseph was restored to him. But Joseph wanted Jacob's right hand on Manasseh's head, for the warmer blessing due to the older son. Jacob moved the two brothers so that his right hand lay on Ephraim's head.

Euphrates River One of the two major rivers running through Babylonia and Mesopotamia—the Tigris was the other.

Fertile Crescent The Fertile Crescent was a strip of land that stretched from Egypt, through Canaan and Mesopotamia, to Babylonia.

Gad One of the original twelve kingdoms of Israel, named after Gad, the first son of Jacob and Zilpah.

Garden of Eden Adam and Eve lived in the Garden of Eden before they were cast out by God. No one knows where the garden was really located.

Gath The place where the giant Goliath lived, before David defeated him.

Gaza After Delilah tricked him, Samson was blinded and thrown into prison in Gaza. When his hair grew back, he destroyed the temple and everyone in it. Gaza is the largest city within the Gaza Strip, an area along the eastern Mediterranean Sea. It was an important trading city in biblical times.

Gilead A mountainous region in the Promised Land, where Jacob and Laban had their last meeting. The Ishmaelites who bought Joseph from his brothers were transporting a substance called "balm of Gilead," a healing ointment made from tree gum.

Goshen When he was reunited with his brothers, Joseph moved them to Goshen in Egypt so that they could escape the famine in Canaan. Israelites remained in Goshen for hundreds of years after that.

Haran Abraham's father had lived in Ur; then he moved his family to Haran. God told Abraham to leave Haran and settle in the promised land of Canaan. Laban stayed in Haran, and there Jacob met and married his cousins Leah and Rachel.

Hebron The Israelites proclaimed David as their new king in Hebron. The name of the town comes from the Hebrew word for "to be joined."

Hezekiah's Tunnel Anticipating an attack by the Assyrians, King Hezekiah of Israel built a remarkable tunnel beneath Jerusalem to protect the city's water supply. The long, sturdy tunnel was a great engineering feat, bringing water from a spring outside the city.

Ishtar Gate The Ishtar Gate was built by King

Nebuchadnezzar. It was the entrance to the Hanging Gardens of Babylon, one of the seven wonders of the ancient world.

Israel The word "Israel" first appears in the Bible as Jacob's new name, given to him by the angel. The

Jerusalem became the Israelites' political and religious center.

name meant "I fight for God," and it eventually came to be used for the land where Jacob and his sons lived. It was divided into twelve kingdoms. Samuel anointed Saul as the first king of Israel. Later, Israel was the name of the northern part of the kingdom, and Judah was the name of the southern part. After 200 years, the Assyrians destroyed Israel.

Issachar One of the original twelve kingdoms of Israel, named for the fifth son of Jacob and Leah. "Leah said, 'God has given me my reward because I gave my maidservant to my husband,' and called him Issachar." (Genesis 30:18)

Jabbok River By the banks of the Jabbok, Jacob wrestled with the angel all night. In the morning, God gave him the name "Israel."

Jabesh When Saul and the Israelite army defeated the Ammonites, they freed the city of Jabesh.

Jericho During the battle of Jericho, as the Israelites claimed the Promised Land, God told Joshua to have the army walk around the city seven times, the priests blow their shofars, and the people shout to the skies. The walls of Jericho fell, and the city belonged to God's people.

Jerusalem David brought the Ark of the Covenant here and made the city the capital of Israel. He fell in love with Bathsheba here, and his son Absalom died near Jerusalem. Later, King Solomon built the First Temple to hold the Ark of the Covenant. Today Jerusalem is the capital of Israel.

Jezreel Valley Saul died in this valley in northern Canaan, near Mount Gilboa.

Jordan An area southeast of Moab.

Jordan River Joshua led his people to the Jordan River, the only thing standing between them and the Promised Land. The river stopped flowing while the men carried the Ark of the Covenant across it. Later, Elijah struck the surface of the river, and the waters divided again.

Judah Judah was originally one of the twelve kingdoms of Israel, named after the fourth son of Jacob and Leah. Judah became a separate country after it divided from Israel when King Solomon died. The country was ruled by Solomon's descendants, starting with his son Rehoboam, until it was conquered by the Babylonians more than 300 years later.

Kidron Valley In the Kidron Valley, the Jews burnt their altars and statues to false gods. King David fled through the valley during Absalom's rebellion.

Lachish During biblical times, Lachish was a stronghold in defending Jerusalem from invasion. To get to Jerusalem, invaders had to approach from the coast and go through Lachish. For many years, the city protected the rest of the country. Then, during Hezekiah's reign, the Assyrians attacked and conquered the city at last, after a fierce battle.

Lake Merom The Jordan River starts at what the Bible calls Lake Merom; today we call it Lake Huleh.

Lebanon In biblical times, Lebanon was home to vast cedar forests. "Cedars of Lebanon" were brought to Jerusalem to build the First Temple.

Manasseh One of the original twelve kingdoms of Israel, named after Joseph's oldest son.

Mediterranean Sea Most of the events in the Bible took place in a small area east of the Mediterranean. It was very important as a way to transport goods and as a source of food. In the Bible, it is sometimes called the Western Sea or just the Great Sea.

Mesopotamia The ancient country of Mesopotamia was located between the upper parts of the Tigris and Euphrates Rivers. Nineveh and Babylon were two of the cities located here.

Midian Fleeing the Pharaoh, Moses arrived in Midian. The Midianites were powerful enemies of the Israelites.

Moab Balak, the king of the Moabites, felt threatened when the Israelites camped on the plains of Moab. He called on Balaam to curse them there, but God would not allow his curses. Moab was also Naomi's home until her husband died.

Moriah God told Abraham to leave his home in Beersheba and travel through the Negev Desert to Moriah. That was the place God had chosen for Abraham to sacrifice his beloved son, Isaac. Abraham followed God's orders. But God's angel let him spare Isaac and instead sacrifice a ram, caught in a thicket.

Mount Ararat After the great flood, Noah's Ark came to rest on a mountain peak in Ararat. Today Ararat is part of Turkey.

Mount Carmel David met Abigail in a ravine near Mount Carmel. And Elijah built an altar to God here, so that He would end the drought.

Mount Gilboa The site of a terrible battle between the Philistines and the Israelites. The Philistines won, and Saul died.

Mount Horeb Mount Horeb is another name for Mount Sinai—see below.

Mount Nebo It is said that Moses died at Mount Nebo, across the river from the Promised Land. The place is sometimes called Mount Pisgah, which means "high place."

Mount Sinai While tending his sheep on Mount Sinai, Moses heard God speaking to him from a burning bush. After three months of wandering, the Israelites camped at the foot of the holy mountain of Sinai. God gave His commandments to Moses here—but when Moses went back down the mountain with the tablets, he found the people worshipping the golden calf.

Nahor At Nahor, a city in Mesopotamia, Abraham's servant found Rebekah at the well outside the city gates. She offered water to him and to his camels, and soon she returned with the servant to marry Isaac.

Naphtali One of the original twelve kingdoms of Israel, named for the second son of Jacob and Bilhah, Rachel's servant. In the struggle between Rachel and Leah to bear sons for Jacob, the children of Rachel's servants counted as victories for Rachel. Naphtali's name, "my struggle," showed how Rachel felt: "With mighty wrestlings have I wrestled with my sister, and have prevailed" (Genesis 30:8).

Nile River Egypt's great river stars in many events of the Bible. It makes its most significance appearance as the home of the bulrushes where baby Moses was hidden, then discovered by Pharaoh's daughter.

Negev Desert The desert in southern Canaan. Beersheba is in the central part of the Negev.

Nimrud A city in Assyria.

Nineveh Nineveh was the capital of Assyria. Jonah ran from Nineveh, trying to escape God's orders, and he was swallowed by a great fish.

Nod After Cain killed Abel, he came to live in the land of Nod, east of the Garden of Eden. The Hebrew word "nod" means "wandering."

Paran Desert Moses had the Israelites camp here while he sent twelve spies to scout the Promised Land.

Persia A huge ancient empire. Esther became Queen of Persia when she married King Ahaseurus.

Pethor Balaam, the fortune teller, lived here, near the Euphrates.

Pithom The Bible says that Pithom was one of the cities built by the pharaoh's Israelite slaves.

Life in Ancient Egypt was centered around the Nile River.

Places in the Bible Stories

Plain of Durah A golden statue was built here, but Daniel's friends refused to worship it.

Ramses The Israelites left this city, which they had built as slaves to Pharaoh, and followed Moses during the Exodus.

Red Sea God showed His power by parting the waters of the Red Sea. The Israelites were able to cross, but their Egyptian pursuers were drowned as the waters returned.

Reuben One of the original twelve kingdoms of Israel, named after the first son of Jacob and Leah. Reuben asked his brothers not to kill Joseph, and later he reminded the others that their problems in Egypt came from their plot to get rid of Joseph.

Samaria King Ahab had his palace here, in the capital of Israel.

Sea of Chinnereth The Sea of Chinnereth is not really a sea—it is actually Israel's largest freshwater lake. It is also called the Sea of Galilee or the Sea of Kinneret.

Sheba A country in southwestern Arabia. Its queen journeyed to see Solomon in Jerusalem.

Shiloh Hannah's prayers at Shiloh were answered when God gave her a son, Samuel. Later, the Philistines stole the Ark of the Covenant from Shiloh.

Shinar An early name for Babylonia.

Shunem In Shunem, Elisha foretold that a woman there would give birth to a boy. Later, he used his staff to bring the boy back to life after the child had died.

Sidon The place where Elijah brought the woman's son back to life.

Simeon One of the original twelve kingdoms of Israel, named for the second son of Jacob and Leah.

Sinai Desert Moses led the Israelites to the Sinai Desert, where God provided manna for them to eat and made water come from a rock.

Sodom and Gomorrah Lot settled in Sodom at the end of Abraham's journey to the Promised Land. But Sodom and Gomorrah became known as evil places, and God rained down fire on them. Only Lot and his family were spared.

Gideon chose men for battle at the Spring of Harod (shown above).

Spring of Harod At the Spring of Harod, Gideon chose the men who would fight against the Midianites.

Succoth Moses and his followers passed through Succoth on their way to the Red Sea.

Syria The country of Syria, north of Israel, was crisscrossed by trade routes and travelers' roads. Its capital is Damascus, one of the oldest continuously occupied cities in the world.

Tigris River One of the two major rivers running through Babylonia and Mesopotamia—the Euphrates was the other.

Timnah In Timnah, Samson fought with a lion and killed it. Later, he found honey in the body.

Tyre Hiram, the king of Tyre, sent cedar wood to Solomon, to use in building the First Temple.

Ugarit A statue of Baal, worshipped by the Canaanites, was found here.

Ur Abraham was born in Ur, in Mesopotamia. He left Ur with his family and moved to Haran, then traveled from Haran to find the Promised Land.

Zebulun One of the original twelve kingdoms of Israel, named for the sixth son of Jacob and Leah.

Zoar Lot's family fled the destruction of Sodom and Gomorrah, escaping to Zoar.

Index

A

Aaron 71, 72, 73, 77, 78, 84, 179
Abed-nego 163–164, 179, 185
Abel 22–23, 179
Abigail 124–125, 179
Abinadab 117, 179
Abraham/Abram 14, 16, 179
    family 30–31, 34–36, 40–45
    journey to Canaan 32–33
    Sodom and Gomorrah 37–39
Absalom 132–133, 179
Adam 20–21, 22, 179
Ahab 142, 144, 179, 186
Ahasuerus 168–171, 179, 185
almond trees 158
altars 115
Ammonites 114
Apis 84
Arab people 41
Arabia 138, 182
Arabian Desert 48, 182
Ararat, Mount 14, 26, 27, 185
Ark of the Covenant 16, 17
    arrival in Jerusalem 128–129,
    130
    at the Battle of Jericho 94–95
    captured by the Philistines
    110–111, 186
    in the Temple of Solomon
    136
Artaxerxes 172
Artaxerxes II 179
Asher (kingdom) 89, 182
Asher (son of Jacob) 30, 53, 179
Ashtoreth (Astarte) 156
Assur 182
Assyria 14, 150, 151, 155, 182

B

Baal 88, 142, 144, 156, 179, 186
Babel 28–29, 182
Babylon 28, 150, 151, 161, 182
Babylonia 150–151, 159, 162,
    182, 186
Balaam 86–87, 179, 185
Balak 86, 87, 179
bar/bat mitzvah 11
baskets 68
bathing 130
Bathsheba 130–131, 179
Beersheba (desert) 182
Beersheba (town) 31, 48, 182
Belshazzar 165, 179
Ben Hinnom 182
Benjamin (kingdom) 89, 182
Benjamin (son of Jacob) 30, 53,
    62, 63, 64–65, 179
Bethel 31, 48, 146, 182
Bethlehem 104, 105, 116, 117,
    182
Bible 10–11
Bible lands 14–15
Bilhah 30
Boaz 105–107, 179
bows and arrows 122, 150, 160
breastpieces 108
Brook of Kerith 140, 182
bulls 84

C

Cain 22–23, 179, 185
Caleb 90, 91, 179

camels 45
Canaan 14, 15, 31, 32–33,
    62, 88–91, 182
Carmel, Mount 143, 148, 185
cedars 136, 186
chariots 61, 146
cherubim 20, 137
children 35
Christianity 11
circumcision 35, 36, 40
cosmetics 168
Creation 18–19
crops 22, 93, 106
cupbearers 59, 172
Cyrus the Great 151, 172,
    179

D

Dagon 110, 111
Damascus 48, 182
Dan (kingdom) 89, 182
Dan (son of Jacob) 30, 53,
    179
dancing 128
Daniel 162–163, 165, 166–
    167, 179
Darius 166–167, 179
David 179
    chosen by God 117
    family 107, 124–125,
    130–133, 135
    and Goliath 118–119
    and Jonathan 122–123
    as King 89, 128–129, 135,
    183
    psalms 176–177

Acknowledgments

Picture Credits

l=left, r=right, t=top, c=center, b=bottom

Ancient Art & Architecture Collection: 60tl.

Ardea: /Wardene Weisser: 80tl.

ASAP: /Aliza Auerbach 14b, 16bc; /Israel Talby 88b.

A−Z Botanical Collection: 136tl.

Barnaby's Picture Library: 54bl.

BBC Radio Vision: 10br, 11tl.

Bijbels Museum, Amsterdam, 1992: 108tl.

Bridgeman Art Library: Whitford and Hughes 8−9; Royal Library Stockholm 10tl.

British Library: 9c.

Trustees of the British Museum: 11c, 20bl, 32bl, 33br, 64tl, 68tl, 68bl, 69tr, 73br, 87br, 101tr, 137br, 146bl, 160cl, 166tl, 167br, 169tr.

Peter Clayton: 65tr.

Bruce Coleman Ltd: 153br.

Professor A. Danin, Jerusalem: 80cl.

Mary Evans Picture Library: 26tl.

Chris Fairclough: 93cr.

Werner Forman Archive: 62tl.

Giraudon: 59br.

Sonia Halliday Photographs: 17bc, 31b, 43tr, 78bl, 83tr, 91br, 95tr, 97tr, 100bl, 105tr, 117tr, 127tr, 135tr, 155tr, 156bl, 157br, 158tl.

Hamburger Kunsthalle: 51tr.

Robert Harding Picture Library: 15bl, 29tr, 50bl, 53tr, 59tr, 61cr, 63cr, 72cl, 76bl, 111tr, 123cr, 148cl, 152tl.

Michael Holford: 58bl, 73tr, 83tr, 132bl, 150b.

Hutchison Picture Library: 11b, 33br, 34tl, 35tr, 51b, 125cr, 139br; /Sarah Errington 52bl.

Image Bank: 128tl; /F. Roiter 131tr; /J. L. Stage 108bl.

Israel Museum, Jerusalem: 11tr; /The Shrine of the Book, D. Samuel & Jeane H. Gottman Center for Biblical Manuscripts 171tr.

Kunsthistorisches Vienna © Mayer: 66t.

Erich Lessing Archive: 99cr, 170bl, 172bl.

Life File: 149tr.

NHPA: /Anthony Bannister 20tl.

Oriental Institute, Chicago: /John Hudson 159br.

Oxford Scientific Films: 45tr.

Planet Earth: /Richard Coomber 141br; /Peter Stephenson 46tl.

Dino Politis: 25br, 29br, 87tr, 173tr.

Zev Radovan: 23tr, 24tl, 27tr, 39br, 40br, 41tr, 119br, 130bl, 133br, 142tl, 143br.

Spectrum Colour Library: 104bl.

Sheila Weir: 45br.

ZEFA: 17br, 42tl, 42bl, 44bl, 66bc, 128bl.

All other images © Dorling Kindersley

for further information, see: **www.dkimages.com**

Dorling Kindersley would like to thank:

Diana Morris and Julia Harris-Voss for picture research; Tim Ridley, Nick Goodall, and Gary Ombler at the DK Studio; Dorian Spencer Davies, Marion Dent, Antonio Forcione, Sally Geeve, Christopher Gillingwater, Polly Goodman, George Hart, Alan Hills, James W. Hunter, Robin Hunter, Marcus James, Fran Jones, Anna Kunst, Michelle de Larrabeiti, Antonio Montoro, Anderley Moore, Jackie Ogburn, Derek Peach, Lenore Person, Dino Politis, Becky Smith, Lara Tankel Holtz, and Martin Wilson for help in producing the original edition; Dr. Eleanor Robson for advice on pp150-1; Karl Stange for sourcing the Hebrew font Peninim; Constance Novis and Jenny Quasha for proof-reading; Maragret Parrish for Americanization; and Sue Lightfoot for the index.

Author acknowledgments:

As it says in Ecclesiastes 12:12, "Of making many books, there is no end; and much study is a weariness of the flesh." Those who helped us to make this book include our dedicated consultants, Rabbi Steven Morgen and Cantor Diane Dorf, and the authors thank them for their thoughtful work. We also want to thank the people at DK who spent so many hours thinking Jewishly about this project: Susan Reuben, Camilla Hallinan, Lisa Stock, Susan St. Louis, and Beth Sutinis. Other friends and teachers who kindly helped us include Dora Geld Friedman, Rabbi Steven Sirbu, and Cantor Ellen Tilem, all from our synagogue, Temple Emeth in Teaneck, New Jersey; Eve Yudelson and Larry Yudelson of Ben Yehuda Press; the librarians at East Rutherford Memorial Library, New Jersey; and Judika Illes, Deborah Brodie, Catherine Reuben, Bryan Reuben, Mella Hort, and our daughters, Sophie, Irene, and Phoebe. Thank you to one and to all!